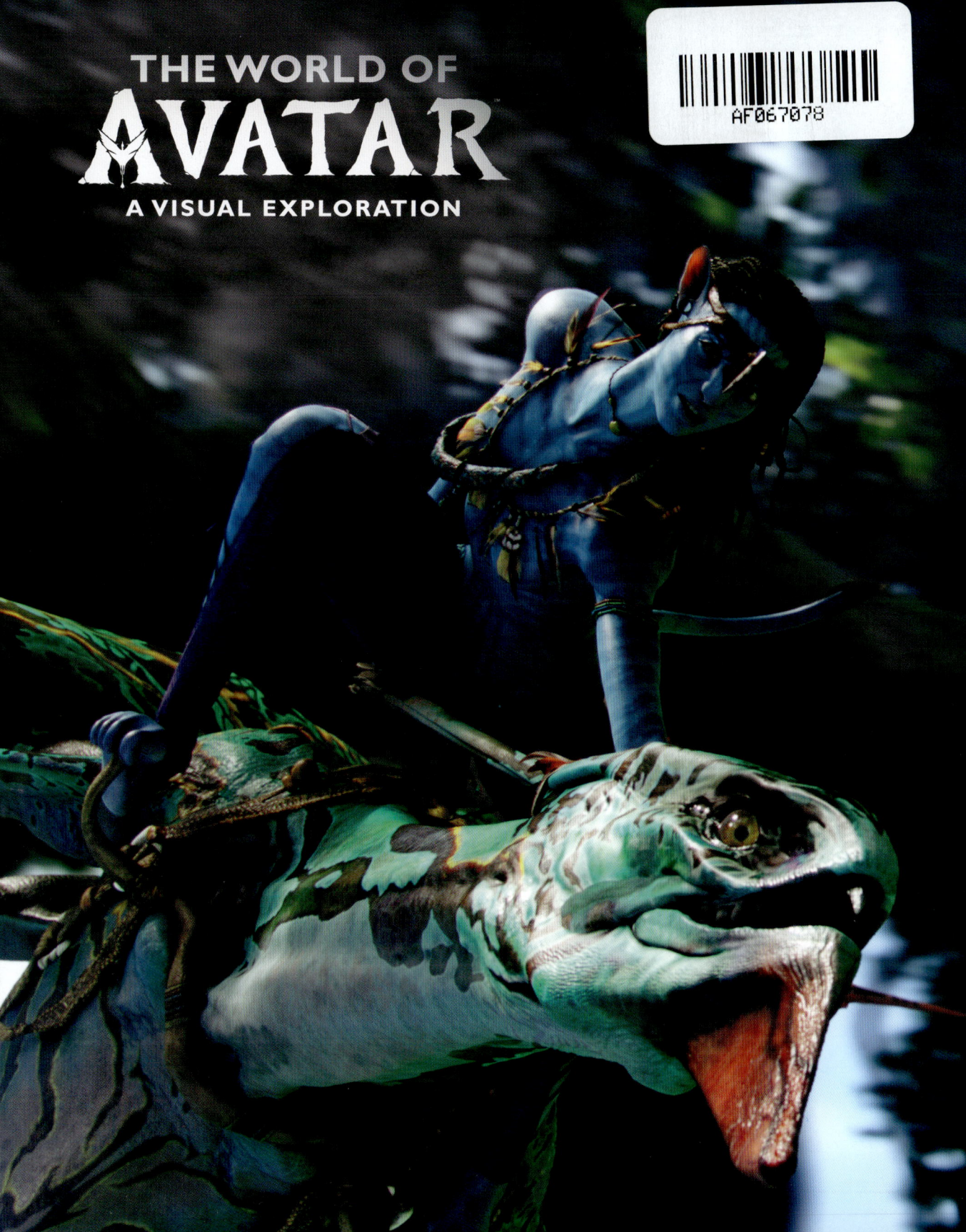

THE WORLD OF AVATAR
A VISUAL EXPLORATION

THE WORLD OF AVATAR

A VISUAL EXPLORATION

BASED ON THE STORY, CHARACTERS,
AND WORLD CREATED BY
JAMES CAMERON

WRITTEN BY
**JOSHUA IZZO, REYMUNDO PEREZ,
AND SIMON BEECROFT**

CONTENTS

Foreword	6
Introduction	8

Chapter One:
THE WORLD OF PANDORA — 10

Pandora	12
Pandora's Geology	14
The Hallelujah Mountains	16
The Rainforest	18
Atolls	20
Diverse Landscapes	22

Chapter Two: FLORA — 24

Trees	26
Plants	28

Chapter Three: FAUNA — 32

Thanator	34
Viperwolf	36
Hammerhead Titanothere	38
Direhorse	40
Land Animals	42
At the Waterhole	48
Great Leonopteryx	50
Mountain Banshee	52
A Warrior's First Hunt	54
Aerial Creatures	56
Aquatic Animals	60
Mounted Warrior	66
Coral and Anemones	68
Tulkun	70

Chapter Four:
THE NA'VI — 72

Na'vi Physiology	74
Na'vi Society	76
Hunting to Live	78
Ocean Life	80
Ceremonies and Rites	82
Na'vi Language	84
History of the Na'vi	86

Chapter Five:
CLANS OF THE NA'VI — 88

Omatikaya Clan	90
Omatikaya Clan Members	92
Sully Family	94
Hometree	96
Inside Hometree	98
High Camp	100
Daily Life	102
Metkayina Clan	104

Na'vi *ilu* riders pass a group of gigantic, bioluminescent nautiloids.

Mangkwan Clan ... 112
Other Na'vi Clans ... 114

Chapter Six:
SACRED SITES ... 122
Na'vi Beliefs ... 124
Eywa's Messengers ... 126
The Tree of Souls ... 128
The Tree of Voices ... 130
Forever Bonded ... 132
The Spirit Tree ... 134

Chapter Seven:
THE RDA ... 136
ISV *Venture Star* ... 138
Return to Pandora ... 140
Valkyrie Shuttle ... 142
Hell's Gate ... 144
An Encroaching Menace ... 146
Bridgehead ... 148
Construction ... 150
Robotic Swarm ... 152
RDA and Sec-Ops Personnel ... 154

AMP Suit Variants ... 164
Skel ... 166
RDA Weaponry ... 168
Aerial Assault ... 172
RDA and Cet-Ops Vehicles ... 174

Chapter Eight:
THE AVATAR PROGRAM ... 176
The Avatar Program ... 178
Science Personnel ... 180
Waking Up ... 182
Science Technology ... 184
Human-Na'vi Programs ... 186
Recom Equipment ... 188

Chapter Nine:
NEW CHALLENGES ... 190
Bridgehead: A New Community ... 192
Factory Ship ... 194
A Battle for Survival ... 196

Index ... 198
Acknowledgments ... 200

FOREWORD

When I first embarked on my *Avatar* journey, I really had no idea what to expect. The story was amazing, the visuals were unlike anything I had ever seen before in my career, and every single part of the world of Pandora was perfectly and exactly crafted—from Pandora herself, to the Na'vi language, to the culture and more. It was absolutely incredible.

In the years since *Avatar* was released I have been blessed with three amazing children. They are my light and I could not think of my life now without them. They've grown up with *Avatar* and know all about Pandora and Neytiri and Jake and the amazing and beautiful alien moon that their mother "lives" on.

When I returned to reprise my role as Neytiri for the *Avatar* sequels, I learned that Neytiri was a mother. My life experience was now experience for stepping back into that role. What I learned during filming was that the story of *Avatar* is really the story of family—and that is something that is relatable to every single person on Earth.

One of the things I did every day with my children was read to them. DK books have been a part of my household forever and when I filmed *Avatar*, I would never in my wildest dreams imagine I would one day be able to share a DK book like this with my family.

It's been an honor and privilege to share this incredible *Avatar* journey with my children, and I hope that you, dear reader, will be able to do the same.

Zoe Saldaña

Zoe Saldaña

INTRODUCTION

I'll never forget reading Jim's *Avatar* scriptment in 1995. Depicted on those pages were some of the most evocative, emotional, and incredibly cinematic ideas that I had ever read. The characters were endearing and relatable. The themes of the story were universal. And the world? Well, simply put, it was amazing—with limitless possibilities.

To create that world cinematically, we engaged the brightest and most creative people we knew. The team included not only some of the film industry's top concept designers, but also an astrophysicist, a professor of botany, a world-renowned painter, a linguist to create the Na'vi language, and many other incredibly talented people. The beautiful and breathtaking world they created revealed only a small section of Pandora and its inhabitants.

Since the initial release of the film, Jim and our team have continued to expand the world of *Avatar*. We have done this through collaborations with Cirque du Soleil on the touring arena show *Toruk: The First Flight*; with Disney Imagineers on the groundbreaking *Pandora: The World of Avatar* at Disney's Animal Kingdom; with Ubisoft on their state-of-the-art PC/Console game *Avatar: Frontiers of Pandora*; and with others in such areas as publishing and location-based entertainment.

With each of these expansions of the *Avatar* universe we added new Na'vi clans and new stories and lore, as well as new creatures and plants to the already rich tapestry created in the film. Which leads me to the book you are holding now.

The World of Avatar: A Visual Journey is a celebration of the *Avatar* universe. The book pulls together threads from various pockets of our known universe and also provides a sneak peek of what will be revealed in our upcoming *Avatar* film sequels. It is my hope that this book not only reminds you of the richness and depth of the *Avatar* world but also provides a tantalizing glimpse of the beauty and majesty yet to be discovered.

As the Na'vi say, "*Irayo*." Thank you. Enjoy your trip back to Pandora.

Jon Landau
Producer

Chapter One

THE WORLD OF PANDORA

PANDORA

4.5 light years from Earth lies the beautiful moon of Pandora, a seemingly unspoiled paradise

The awe-inspiring, magical beauty of Pandora and the mysteries of its Na'vi inhabitants, flora, and fauna are more than enough to fire the imagination of a visitor from Earth. Indeed, the discovery of this primal paradise 4.5 light years away has contributed to a seismic shift in humankind's perception of our place in the universe and relationship with our own fragile planet.

Pandora possesses natural beauty surpassing anything on Earth. At night, almost every living thing blazes with bioluminescence—an enthralling, flashing, flickering, rainbow-hued display. On a spiritual level, a strange harmony pervades all Pandoran life. Humans that embrace it experience a sense of peace and belonging unlike anything they have ever known before.

Yet no paradise is perfect. Pandora experiences enormous volcanic eruptions as well as magnetic storms, caused by interactions with the magnetic field of neighboring gas giant Polyphemus. It also has a number of dangerous, even deadly, plants and animals.

Polyphemus
In the skies above Pandora looms the gas giant planet Polyphemus. Roughly twice the size of Neptune, Polyphemus has 14 moons, of which Pandora is the fifth closest.

Uncharted territory
Pandora is covered in massive oceans and continents, most of which remain totally unexplored by humans.

A DECEIVING PARADISE

Pandora is similar in size and appearance to Earth and has lush forests, spectacular mountains, valleys, plains, lakes, rivers, islands, and continents surrounded by seas.

But Pandora is not Earth. Its nitrogen-oxygen atmosphere is much denser than our own and contains so much carbon dioxide that humans who breathe it soon become unconscious and die. Another toxic gas, hydrogen sulfide, is spewed out by hundreds of continually erupting volcanoes.

The moon's plant life often contains chemicals that render it unfit for human consumption, while many species have poisonous thorns or pods that explode and spray acidic sap.

Data file

NA'VI NAME: *Eywa'eveng* or "*Eywa*'s Child"

ENVIRONMENT: Earth-like, but humans need an exomask to breathe its air.

RESOURCES: The only known source of unobtanium, vital to Earth's economy, and *amrita*, which halts human aging.

PANDORA'S GEOLOGY

Alien and beautiful, the extraordinary geology of Pandora is a world unto itself

Strong gravitational influences from Polyphemus, Pandora's gas giant parent planet, have brought about a variety of bizarre, electromagnetically derived phenomena. Unobtanium ore within rock formations such as the Hallelujah Mountains and the stone arches has resulted in some of these huge masses literally floating—suspended between the powerful, overlapping magnetic forces of Pandora and Polyphemus.

Such magnetic field anomalies exist at several sites. There are a number of fluxcons (flux concentrations) dotted around Pandora, including the Flux Vortex that lifts the Hallelujah Mountains. A countering form of magnetism—flux pinning (aka quantum locking)—stops the mountains from being literally pulled into space.

Torus-shaped feature
The huge, arching structure at the Cove of the Ancestors is a spectacular example of a fluxcon.

COVE OF THE ANCESTORS

The sacred site of the Metkayina clan, the Cove of the Ancestors, is a flux concentration with an exceptionally powerful magnetic field and strong concentrations of unobtanium. Relatively small horizontal floating islands are flux-pinned in space here, above, and below the water.

UNOBTANIUM

One of the main reasons that humans established a base of operations on such a distant moon is to mine the precious ore unobtanium. Unique to Pandora, unobtanium is a rare-earth compound and "high-temperature" superconductor and has become the backbone of Earth's economy. Unobtanium is used by many specialized applications, such as Superluminal Communications and computer hyperchip manufacturing. The ore sells for close to $44 million per pound ($20 million per kilogram).

Precious and rare
A small, but highly valuable and sought-after sample of unobtanium floats in a Resources Development Administration (RDA) magnetic containment field.

Magnetic majesty
Malmok or "Rings of Stone" were formed when Pandora cooled from its molten state. Magnetic fields shaped the molten rock, which then hardened. Over millennia, wind and weather have eroded the rock to form spectacular arches.

THE HALLELUJAH MOUNTAINS

The majestic, mysterious *Ayram Alusìng* hover high among the clouds

The magnificent, spectacular Hallelujah Mountains—just one of the many different floating mountain ranges on Pandora—are composed of billions of tons of rock that float high in the air like clouds. The mountains are heavily forested and often have majestic waterfalls cascading down their sheer sides. These massive rock formations are connected by great cable-like bridges of vegetation.

High winds and storms sometimes cause the mountains to collide in midair. These crushing impacts have led the Na'vi to call these marvels *Ayram Alusìng* or "Thundering Rocks." The mountains seem to defy gravity, but the scientific explanation for them derives from Pandora's liquid iron core and its proximity to the planet Polyphemus. The combination of Pandora's denser atmosphere, the magnetic pull of Polyphemus, and large rocks rich in superconducting unobtanium ore creates these floating wonders.

Sky high
Jake Sully and members of his family ride their *ikran* between the Hallelujah Mountains.

Hazardous flying conditions
Magnetic fields that suspend the mountains disrupt radar. Pilots have to rely on their eyesight to navigate through clouds and avoid collisions.

Natural attachment
Smaller floating rock clusters form alongside these vast mountains. Boulders are tethered to each other only by the vines that grow between them.

Sacred sites in the sky
The mountains are the staging ground for *Iknimaya*, one of a series of dangerous rites of passage in which a young Na'vi warrior must select (and be selected by) and then bond with one of the mountain banshees who roost there.

FLOATING MOUNTAINS

Floating mountains and stone arches are two of Pandora's most distinctive landforms. Both are markers for the presence of the invaluable mineral unobtanium, which, owing to the high concentration of magnetic polarization, causes considerable disruption to human technology. The mountains serve as a highly visible warning to pilots of the nexus of intense magnetic fields. The first human explorers to see the floating mountains were awestruck (as are all humans lucky enough to have seen the phenomenon). The sight of billions of tons of rock floating as weightlessly as clouds seemed utterly inexplicable. When these explorers returned to base, their comrades thought that the holographic images they brought back were an elaborate practical joke.

Beautiful but dangerous
By day, the slanting rays of Pandora's sun illuminate a profusion of strange, exotic plants.

Hometree rising
Of all the immense trees in the rainforest, the Omatikaya Hometree is one of the oldest and largest.

THE RAINFOREST

The Omatikaya clan of the Na'vi make their home in one of Pandora's many immense rainforests

Na'ring is the great rainforest closest to where the human "Sky People" build their Hell's Gate colony. As with many of Pandora's biological phenomena, the forest is laced with bioluminescent flora that glow in darkness. Many of the rainforest's trees are so tall they almost seem to reach up to the sky. Although a bountiful-seeming paradise, nearly every area of the forest contains a plant, animal, or geological feature that may spell danger—even death—to unwary strangers. It is in this forest, among the jellyfish-like panopyra, succulent dapophet, and iridescent warbonnet ferns, that the human explorers of Pandora first encounter creatures like the mighty titanothere and the vicious viperwolf. With the Omatikaya people as their guides, these humans learn that although peril may lurk around every tree, great beauty may also be found in the smallest of wonders.

A WONDERFUL WILDERNESS

Every layer of the vast rainforest teems with life. Its magnificent trees are ten times larger than any found on Earth. A typical Na'vi can walk, run, even ride a heavy direhorse across the elevated root system that crisscrosses the mid-canopy level. The ground is filled with other plants and insects and with a host of animals of all sizes and shapes. The upper canopies are home to numerous creatures of the air, such as the forest banshee and tetrapteron.

The rainforest at night
Glowing panopyra illuminate the rainforest. The zooplantae (part animal, part plant) lifeforms of Pandora—like the panopyra and helicoradian—have primitive nervous systems. Panopyra grows toward its prey, unaffected by gravity.

Rich waters
The shallows of the tranquil lagoon are full of unique fish brought in from the ocean by the upward water flows.

ATOLLS

The Metkayina's island home is protected by a seawall that the clan believes was created by *Eywa*

Na'vi sea cultures, or "Reef People," are closely aligned to the rhythms and wildlife of Pandora's oceans where they make their homes. The Metkayina live on an island among atolls and coastal and barrier reefs, which form a natural seawall that encloses a calm lagoon. They built their villages among enormous mangrove-like trees that fringe the island. In every way, Metkayina life is tied to their beloved rich marine habitat.

Although relations with other clans are currently peaceful, the Metkayina maintain their reputation as fierce warriors who would die to protect their home. Though they were too remote to fight alongside the Omatikaya in the first battle against the Sky People, the RDA's return—and the Sully family's surprise appearance—threatens their existence.

UNIQUE REEF

The Metkayina live within an atoll, with a ring-shaped seawall approximately 30 miles (48 km) in diameter. The tide flows in and out through openings in the wall structure, welling up and cascading down to form terraced tide pools, which are unique to Pandoran reefs. Over millions of years, the corals on the barrier reef have grown up to 100 ft (30.5 m) above the surface of the water, quite unlike any coral reefs found on Earth.

Worlds apart
The atoll is approximately 300 miles (483 km) northeast of the Omatikaya rainforest, or an eight-hour flight by *ikran*, including rest stops.

DIVERSE LANDSCAPES

Exploring offshore regions of the Omatikaya and the topography of the Western Frontier

Pandora's continents, islands, oceans, and seas are home to a wide variety of environments inhabited by Na'vi clans, from the rainforest-dwelling Omatikaya to the oceanic Metkayina, and countless species of animals and plants. The RDA has focused attention on the moon's Western Frontier, located on a separate continent from the Omatikaya, which has a wealth of natural resources and is home to many clans, including the Aranahe, Sarentu, Zeswa, and Kame'tire. The region includes the dense jungle of the Kinglor Forest; the mountainous Clouded Forest, rich in pine trees, mosses, and fungi; and the Upper Plains, notable for their grasslands, colorful flora, lush grasses, caves, and stark rock formations.

Upper Plains
The region of the Western Frontier known as the Upper Plains is mostly windswept grasslands with cliffs and soaring stone arches. It is home to the fierce Zeswa clan, who roam the area along with animals such as *kxaylkxa* (bladeheads).

Abundant lands
The Western Frontier is rich in natural gases and fuels, which makes it a target for exploitation by the RDA's Frontier Operations.

Kinglor Forest
The Western Frontier's Kinglor Forest is a rainforest with great roots and wild, twisting vines. It is home to the artistic Aranahe clan and fauna such as hammerhead titanotheres, hexapedes, and *kinglors*—the large, moth-like creatures that give this forest its name.

The Spires
Located in the Western Frontier's Clouded Forest, the Spires is a region of steep rocky landscapes inhabited by predators called echo stalkers, who hunt using echolocation.

Tranquil forest
The Clouded Forest, with its towering trees, rocky gorges, and natural caves, is home to the rare and magnificent sailfin goliath.

Chapter Two
FLORA

TREES

Pandora's rainforests contain a bewildering variety of amazing species

Human xenobotanists such as Dr. Grace Augustine have spent years studying the trees of Pandora's rainforest. There may be as many as a 100,000 different species. Based on the current level of study, it would take centuries to identify and classify each one.

The Na'vi, on the other hand, possess an intimate knowledge of every single tree in the rainforests. They know precisely which ones are safe, which are poisonous, which are good for repelling bugs, which hold water, and which bear the tastiest fruit.

Panopyra
The Na'vi regard the liquid that collects in the panopyra's cup-like body as a nutritious and healing drink. Its flexible stems are used for making nets, traps, and other woven items.

Celia fruit tree
The berry pistil contains up to 100 berries and usually ends with a single large one that is the most delicious. It is often fought over by Na'vi children harvesting the fruit.

Episoth tree
This tree produces abundant flowers and large, spiny fruits. These fruits explode, dispersing hundreds of seeds that stick to anything they come in contact with.

Unidelta tree
This comparatively small tree has large, bioluminescent leaves and roots that also grow above ground. These contain a toxin that kills and digests invertebrates.

Lizard tree
This tree is so named by xenobotanists for its distinctive iridescent, blue-green bark, which resembles the scales of a terran lizard.

Fountain tree
This relatively small rainforest succulent is crowned by densely leafed branches terminating in bulbous, fluid-filled fruit.

Cannonball tree
To harvest the fruit, the Na'vi climb to the top of the tree and launch it from the highest branch. With the right velocity, the husk cracks when it hits the ground and the Na'vi then insert sharpened branches and split it to reveal the fruit inside.

Squid fruit tree
The fruits of this tall tree are a staple of the Na'vi diet. Its seedpods, which are covered in blue, spiny protrusions, hang from long, tentacle-like stalks.

Razor palm
The branches of this tall tree have narrow, strap-like leaves. Its bark is covered with sharp, razor-like spines. The Na'vi call it *pxiut* or "sharp tree."

Carnivorous

Like Earth's Venus flytrap, some plants on Pandora take sustenance from insects, and even creatures as large as fan lizards.

Leaf pitcher
Insects attracted by its nectar are trapped in its coiling leaves and digested.

Chalice plant
This large, pitcher-shaped plant has abundant nectar to entice small animals.

Dakteron
Vine with elaborate modified leaf for trapping insects. Showy flower has bulbous, coral-like structure that emits fragrance to lure insects.

Anemonoid
Large forest herb with hair-like leaves traps insects in its sticky, flat top. Unique among Pandoran plants, it absorbs small amounts of unobtanium from the soil.

Zooplantae

These are a unique Pandoran plant type. They are "sentient" in the sense that they have a rudimentary nervous system.

Cat ear
This "planimal" has the uncanny ability to turn toward an animal moving through the rainforest.

Helicoradian
Responds to touch by coiling and retracting rapidly into the ground. Often grows in clusters, where movement of one plant triggers all to retract.

Binary sunshine
These plants detect danger by sensing the emission of stress hormones from living organisms.

Grub plant
A favorite food of many creatures. Sensory cells in its leaves respond to the smell of animals and the plant retracts in defense.

Twisted lily
Its leaves' sensory cells detect a living creature and react by slapping it if it comes too close.

Ferns

Much like ferns on Earth, these species can grow to immense proportions. They have a variety of daily uses for the Na'vi.

Thistle bud
The large seeds of this plant are a Na'vi food staple. When the seeds are mature, the Na'vi use a stick to whack the stem to the ground, allowing the seeds to be easily collected. Whoever is collecting the seeds often has to compete with animals, which also find them a valuable food.

Canalyd
The plant's leathery stem functions as a defense mechanism to prevent animals eating it. The Na'vi use it to make saddles, belts, containers, and other artifacts.

Warbonnet fern
The special pattern of bioluminescence in its rays lures insects to feed on its nectar. The Na'vi use the leaves for illumination and also to make spectacular headdresses.

PLANTS

The ground-level plant life of Pandora is diverse, often beautiful, sometimes dangerous

Some of Pandora's plant life resembles that on Earth, but much of it is unique to this world. The diversity of plants suggests that, as on Earth, the environment on Pandora acts as a strong force for natural selection. The environmental factors that plants experience on Earth—radiation, water, atmospheric gases, and gravity—are present on Pandora. However, Pandora's atmosphere is denser than Earth's, with higher concentrations of carbon dioxide, as well as hydrogen sulfide and xenon. Gravity is weaker, while the moon's magnetic field is incredibly strong. These factors have contributed to plant evolution, making most Pandoran plants considerably larger than those of Earth. In addition, the typical orientation found on Earth—stems growing up and roots growing down—does not necessarily hold true on Pandora.

Vein pod
Absorbs methane from the air, giving it a noxious smell. When its globular structures reach maximum capacity they float away, exploding high in the sky.

Goblin thistle
Fungus-like blooms along the trunk have the same properties as terran bacitracin and are a natural antibiotic balm or salve.

Scorpion thistle
Its single flower exudes an acidic liquid that clears the soil below the plant and promotes germination of its seeds.

Banshee of paradise
Wind blowing through its tubular body creates an eerie wailing sound. Detects warmth from organisms and rotates toward them. Shoots poison-tipped spines as defense.

Cillaphant
Attracted to magnetic fields, which, for unknown reasons, may cause the plant to eject the tips of its tubular leaves. They are sharp enough to cause serious injury.

Flaska reclinata
The flaska reclinata is one of the most important plants on Pandora. It plays an important role on the moon by helping to detoxify the atmosphere.

Plants of the Western Frontier

The Western Frontier's Upper Plains and Clouded Forest are home to plants with a variety of survival mechanisms, as well as species that provide sustenance to the Na'vi who live here.

Cloud spitter
Growing on grasslands, the cloud spitter is so-named for the way its flower "explodes" and disperses seeds in a long, high arc.

Feather blade
The hardy feather blade grows in the windswept Upper Plains. The Na'vi dry its stamens and use them for sweet-smelling kindling. They also cook with the plant's large, starchy seeds.

Sunflower gigantus
A large, nutrient-rich plant, the sunflower gigantus can release the energy stored in its stems and propel anything that steps on it a great distance into the air.

Mist bloom
Native to grasslands and rainforests, the mist bloom grows on the ground or on vines. It emits a cloud of seed spores when disturbed.

Mermaid tail
The leafy body of this plant lies across the ground but can spring to an upward position if disturbed—an action that deters predators.

Lift vine
This carnivorous plant grows in high places such as tall vines and cliff edges. Its trailing vine can trap and pull up insects to its digestive core.

Hardy survivors
Many species are adapted for life in the Western Frontier's prairie-like Upper Plains and temperate Clouded Forest.

Banshee's tail
Adapted to the exposed plains, this plant has leathery leaves and deep roots. Its appendages resemble the tail of a banshee.

Phalanxia
Known to the Na'vi as *smaoe*, the phalanxia is covered in sharp spines. The plant can eject these spines like projectiles, using gas that collects in specialized bladders within its trunk.

Rain thistle
During rainstorms, the rain thistle opens to reveal its seedpod. Adapted to rocky terrain, it stores water in its fibers.

Eyethorn
This planimal can detect the presence of nearby organisms and sway its body in a violent jutting motion to deter them.

Chapter Three
FAUNA

Data file

NA'VI NAME: *Palulukan*

HABITAT: Rainforests; subarctic regions

ANATOMY: Armored head with ten sensory quills; massive jaw with teeth 9 in (23 cm) long; armored tail and back.

LENGTH: 18 ft (5.5 m)

HEIGHT: 8 ft 3 in (2.5 m)

THANATOR

The rainforest's most fearsome predator strikes terror wherever it roams

This powerful animal rules over its territory. The Omatikaya, who are renowned for their courage, are shaken by the thanator's approach, and do not celebrate it in dance or song. No wonder Dr. Grace Augustine tells the inexperienced Jake Sully's avatar—whose shots bounce harmlessly off the thanator's armored hide and just further enrage it—to run for his life.

The thanator's senses are so highly developed that it can detect prey up to 8 miles (13 km) away. As well as possessing hugely powerful jaws filled with long, razor-sharp teeth perfect for tearing flesh, it can also deliver a lethal blow with its armored tail. Furthermore, anything a thanator decides to chase down has little chance, as it is also one of Pandora's fastest land animals. Its six legs can propel it at speeds of up to 40 mph (64 kph) in short bursts, and it is also incredibly agile—Jake only manages to escape the creature's jaws by lucky accident, falling from a high cliff into a river.

Hunter and prey
As soon as the deadly thanator senses potential prey, it raises its distinctive crest and gets ready to pounce.

APEX PREDATOR

A thanator usually hunts alone and does not stray outside its territory, which is believed to be roughly 186 sq miles (482 sq km). It hunts mainly at night, unless it is particularly hungry.

Perhaps the animal's most unusual feature is its crest of ten sensory quills, two sprouting from each armor plate encircling the back of its skull. The function of these quills is not fully understood; they may be a threat display and also a sensory aid that helps the thanator pinpoint the location of its prey.

Data file

NA'VI NAME: *Nantang*

HABITAT: Rainforests; grasslands

ANATOMY: Six legs; four eyes; hairless; armor plating around neck and on spine; signs of evolving from a dog-like creature to a simian one; paws have opposable thumbs.

LENGTH: 7 ft 6 in (2.3 m)

HEIGHT: 3 ft 3 in (1 m)

VIPERWOLF

Packs of these ravening, sharp-toothed creatures stalk the rainforest floor

With six legs and lean, powerful torsos, viperwolves can travel swiftly over long distances in search of prey. Their keen, intelligent green eyes can see as clearly at night as in the day. Their sense of smell is awesome. It is believed they can sense prey at a distance of 5 miles (8 km). When stalking prey, the viperwolf hugs the ground or clings to a tree branch with its primate-like paws. Thus hidden, a viperwolf can often approach close to its unsuspecting prey and attack with frightening efficiency.

Apart from the mountain banshee and thanator, few predators will attack a viperwolf, which usually lives in packs of 10 to 12 animals. The pack can turn into a highly cooperative hunting party in seconds, communicating with barks, yelps, facial tics, and paw gestures.

Family feeling
A mother viperwolf tends to her pups with all the care and devotion of a female wolf on Earth.

LIFE IN THE PACK

Viperwolves patrol their territory fiercely, scent-marking, hunting, and guarding against any incursion, especially by rival viperwolf packs. Some of the pack guard expectant mothers in safe forest dens. A few months after birth, a viperwolf cub has to learn to hunt. Fortunately, cubs mature swiftly, growing to half adult size by six months. By then, they have a full set of teeth and their jaw muscles are almost mature. A viperwolf's jaws can exert 9 lbs per sq in (0.6 kg per sq cm) of pressure, easily enough to crush bone.

HAMMERHEAD TITANOTHERE

Giant of the Pandoran rainforests

Nearly twice the size of an African elephant, and much faster, these massive, six-limbed, herbivorous grazing creatures travel in small herds, each led by a dominant alpha bull. Despite possessing four eyes, titanotheres have weak eyesight. However, their senses of smell and hearing are excellent, detecting danger in an instant. When a titanothere is angered or feels threatened, it raises its purple crest, lowers its head, and charges, crushing anything in its path. The sheer ferocity of a titanothere charge is usually enough to send any other Pandoran creature running. Among their own species, titanotheres are extremely territorial and rival bulls frequently engage in spectacular battles. Alpha males spread their scent by smashing trees to pulp, warning other animals (especially other bulls) to steer well clear.

Face to face
Jake Sully's avatar's first, unforgettable contact with the strange native fauna of Pandora is with an enraged titanothere.

HEAD FIRST

The imposing hammerhead structure projecting from the titanothere's head is formed of cartilage rather than bone. A young titanothere's hammerhead is flexible enough to allow the animal to pass through quite tight gaps, enabling it to shelter in dense jungle. However, as the creature matures, its hammerhead becomes as solid as bone. Swinging their heads from side to side, bulls will attempt to injure their opponents' eyes with the ends of their hammers. For extra protection in such fights, the titanothere's tank-like body has overlapping bony plates on its shoulders and back.

Data file

NA'VI NAME: *Angtsìk*
HABITAT: Rainforests; open grasslands
ANATOMY: Six legs; four eyes; massive, low-slung head with bony projections on either side of the skull; mouth protected by a rigid, beak-like jaw.
LENGTH: 36 ft (11 m)
HEIGHT: 19 ft 8 in (6 m)

Danger sign
When threatened, a titanothere raises its crest, made up of brightly colored flaps of skin. It also uses its crest to attract a mate.

DIREHORSE

Noble, six-legged steed of the Na'vi

The *pa'li*, or direhorse, is vitally important as a mode of transport and mount for hunting for all Na'vi clans. With its six legs, the direhorse is superbly adapted to riding speedily over rugged terrain or through an obstacle-strewn forest. Direhorses can turn on a dime, have excellent reactions, and can leap long distances with ease.

Direhorses are tamed—often with some difficulty—when the would-be rider forms a neural link, known as *tsaheylu*, with the animal. Once this is achieved, a Na'vi rider can communicate directions and commands instantly, almost as if the direhorse was an extension of the rider's own body. This frees up the Na'vi to use a bow and arrow during a hunt or battle. The neural link made between rider and direhorse does not lead to a lifelong, exclusive bond between Na'vi and animal; although Na'vi have their favorite mounts, it is possible and permissible to ride another clan member's direhorse.

Favorite food
The direhorse's long, thin tongue is perfectly adapted to reach the sweet nectar of the direhorse pitcher plant.

Forging a bond
A Na'vi rider forms a neural link by connecting their *kuru* with one of the direhorse's.

Data file

NA'VI NAME: *Pa'li*
HABITAT: Rainforests and grasslands, but adaptable to most Pandoran environments.
ANATOMY: Horse-like creature with six legs; four eyes; tough skin with no fur; long neck and small head; bold stripes; flexible carbon-fiber armor over shoulders and the back of neck and head.
LENGTH: 13 ft 10 in (4.23 m)
HEIGHT: 13 ft 8 in (4.2 m)

PA'LI IN THE WILD

In the wild, direhorses gather in loose herds of up to a hundred animals to feed on tree bark and shrubs. Herds often move in unison shortly after the animals have touched *kuru*—two long, thin antennae on either side of their head. These *kuru* have feathery tips that constantly move and seek out the *kuru* of other direhorses as they come near.

Xenobiologists believe that the touch of these antennae is for pleasure and affection, and is also a means of transferring information about food sources and potential dangers.

LAND ANIMALS

Pandoran wildlife has evolved in all sorts of spectacular ways

Pandora is home to a wide variety of creatures that walk, run, fly, and shuffle about the floor of the moon's rainforests. Some of these animals—such as the monkey-like prolemuris or the poisonous arachnoid—are a nuisance to the Na'vi. The prolemuris' treetop chattering warns other animals of an approaching hunter, while the arachnoid packs a powerful sting in its tail that can be fatal. The docile tapirus, on the other hand, can be domesticated, thus becoming a valuable food source and sometimes a pet. The massive sturmbeest and the shy hexapede are also staples of the Na'vi diet and prime targets for hunting parties. Each of these creatures plays a vital role in the ecological system of the rainforest, often as prey for ferocious predators such as the viperwolf and thanator.

Hexapede
This beautiful, agile herbivore, called *yerik* by the Na'vi, has highly attuned senses but few other defenses to ward off predators. However, retractable fans on the top of its head can distract attackers and add a little extra height. An adult can stand up to 7 ft 6 in (2.3 m) from fan-tip to toe. The *yerik* is the first animal that a would-be Na'vi warrior is allowed to kill, marking their transition from child to adult.

Slinger
The slinger's unusual hunting method involves the head completely detaching from its body and flying toward its prey. Once the venomous head penetrates its target, it emits a high-pitched noise for the body to follow. The head and body reconnect using an internal *kuru*. The two parts of the slinger are actually a parent and child in a symbiotic relationship. Once the head is fully grown, it detaches and mates. It then metamorphoses into a smaller slinger, with its own offspring head. Unable to feed, the original parent body dies.

Crested porcuboar
Found in the Anurai clan's rainforest region (see pp. 116–17), the crested porcuboar is 4 ft (1.5 m) high and 8 ft (2.5 m) long. The sharp spikes on the head and hindquarters can be shot at enemies, using the animal's powerful muscular system. These spikes are prized by Na'vi in headdress decoration.

Slinth

The slinth spends most of its day sleeping in the lower canopy of the rainforest. However, when it wakes to feed, it is one of the fastest land animals on Pandora. The slinth injects its prey with a powerful neurotoxin before eating it alive. The Na'vi have perfected a non-harmful way to extract slinth venom and use it for medicinal purposes.

Protective plates

The slinth's face is normally covered by four segments of hard plate. These protect the slinth's fangs when closed, but open to create a bright threat display.

Sturmbeest

These hefty, six-legged animals can weigh up to 1,984 lbs (900 kg) and reach 23 ft (7 m) in height. Their eyesight is poor, but their other senses are extremely acute. They can smell a predator more than 2 miles (3 km) away. Sturmbeest are herd animals and groups will stampede if alarmed.

Cuirass crab

These massive crabs scuttle across the rainforest floor on their 20 multi-jointed legs. The crab is protected from predators by an incredibly hard shell, which can reach up to 5 ft (1.5 m) in diameter, and a tail that is covered in sharp quills.

Fan lizard

Pandora has weaker gravity and denser air than Earth, so the rapid opening of the lizard's fan lifts it rapidly into the air and away from danger. When unfurled, the fan lizard stretches over 3 ft 4 in (1 m) in diameter.

Cuirass mud crab

This sub-species of the cuirass crab, with distinctive terracotta and green markings, lives near rivers, lakes, and swamps. They group together in colonies on tree branches and trunks for protection.

Flight of the fan lizard

Na'vi children enjoy disturbing resting fan lizards, and then marveling as these luminous magenta-and-purple discs float away to safety.

Austrapede

The austrapede stands an impressive 13 ft (4 m) tall, but poses little threat to most creatures. Unlike Pandora's other bird-like fauna, the lofty austrapede's wings have devolved into vestigial appendages, like those of an emu. It flaps its wings when it is frightened. These peaceful creatures laze about the riverbeds and rivers of Pandora.

Wolf tick

A wolf tick survives by feeding off the blood of a large animal like the hammerhead titanothere or sturmbeest. The tick embeds its head and thorax in the host using its powerful mandibles and sharp barbs. If left undisturbed, these parasites can stay attached and feeding for up to eight days.

Arachnoid

Scorpion-like arachnoids are plentiful on Pandora. The venom of one species, the *kali'weya*, is used in the Na'vi's Dream Hunt ceremony.

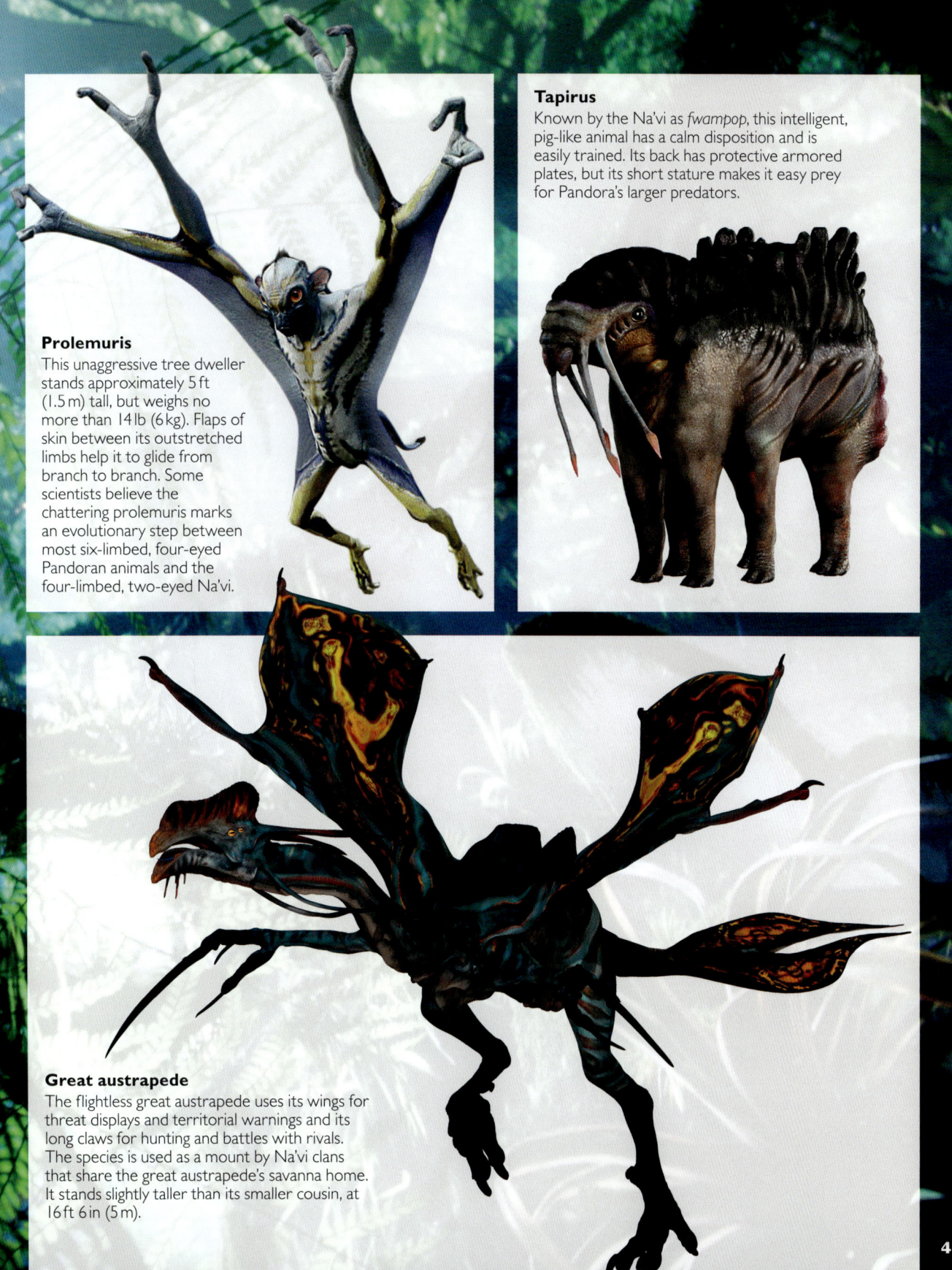

Prolemuris
This unaggressive tree dweller stands approximately 5 ft (1.5 m) tall, but weighs no more than 14 lb (6 kg). Flaps of skin between its outstretched limbs help it to glide from branch to branch. Some scientists believe the chattering prolemuris marks an evolutionary step between most six-limbed, four-eyed Pandoran animals and the four-limbed, two-eyed Na'vi.

Tapirus
Known by the Na'vi as *fwampop*, this intelligent, pig-like animal has a calm disposition and is easily trained. Its back has protective armored plates, but its short stature makes it easy prey for Pandora's larger predators.

Great austrapede
The flightless great austrapede uses its wings for threat displays and territorial warnings and its long claws for hunting and battles with rivals. The species is used as a mount by Na'vi clans that share the great austrapede's savanna home. It stands slightly taller than its smaller cousin, at 16 ft 6 in (5 m).

Chameleon crawler
Native to the Western Frontier's Clouded Forest, this small predator hunts in packs and can change its skin color for camouflage.

Cloaked Panther
In the Western Frontier's Upper Plains, the cloaked panther uses its wing-shaped membrane to glide into an attack on prey.

Echo stalker
Adapted for life in the fog of the Clouded Forest, the blind *mimikyun*, or echo stalker, uses a complex system of multiple ears to seek out prey using echolocation.

Sailfin goliath
The Clouded Forest-dwelling sailfin goliath is a rare and solitary beast. Non-aggressive and slow-moving, it tends a garden of planimals (plant/animal hybrids) and uses its long tendrils to waft pollen around.

Zakru
The Western Frontier's largest megafauna uses its trunk to feed on colonies of microorganisms found beneath the soil.

Soundblast colossus
This large creature uses its crest to catch winds on the Western Frontier's Upper Plains. It releases these winds in a wave of intense sound that deters predators.

Beetlehorn ursabrute
This carnivore is 13 ft (4 m) in height, has few natural predators, and has been known to hurl boulders at its enemies to weaken them. As the animal ages, the horns on its head grow larger and become more complex in shape.

AT THE WATERHOLE

A group of sturmbeest crosses a wide patch of marshy terrain to drink and wallow in the cool mud, before moving on to another feeding location. These massive creatures form large herds and are highly protective of their young. The Na'vi sustainably hunt these animals for meat and various byproducts.

Data file

NA'VI NAME: *Toruk*
HABITAT: Mountain aeries
ANATOMY: Huge, leathery wings; immensely strong, carbon-fiber skeleton; massive talons; twin tail aids agility in flight; sharp, bony crest; four eyes.
COLORATION: Scarlet-yellow-and-black-striped body, head, and wings; dark blue crest.
WINGSPAN: Up to 102 ft (31 m)

A terrifying sight
The *toruk*'s jaw structure enables its mouth to open extremely wide, exposing rows of razor-sharp, bayonet-like teeth.

GREAT LEONOPTERYX

Apex predator of the Pandoran skies

Toruk, the Na'vi name for this creature, translates as "last shadow," reflecting the belief that if this magnificent flying carnivore casts its shadow over you, that shadow will be the last you ever see. The *toruk*'s preferred prey are mountain banshees. However, this solo hunter has also been known to attack aircraft piloted by humans, probably believing that these strange vehicles pose a threat to its supremacy in the air. The Na'vi regard the *toruk* as one of *Eywa*'s greatest creations. The animal is honored in the Hometree of the Omatikaya clan by a totem built around a *toruk* skull. Ceremonial dances and songs endow the *toruk* with mythic power and significance and reflect the Na'vi's fear and respect for the species. The few humans lucky enough to have survived seeing a *toruk* on the wing can only marvel at the creature's grace and command of the Pandoran sky.

Majestic savior
An ancient Na'vi story relates how the giant *toruk* once helped to save the Tree of Souls from a natural disaster. Believing that riding on a *toruk*—a feat that had never been accomplished before—was the only way to avert the disaster, a group of young Na'vi searched for the *toruk* in its mountain home.

CREATURE OF LEGEND
In rare instances, one of the Na'vi manages to link with a *toruk*. This has only happened during tumultuous eras. The Na'vi who accomplishes this is given the title *Toruk Makto* or "Rider of the Last Shadow." Only someone with a pure soul can ride a *toruk*; some brave but foolish Na'vi have tried to link with one and perished. It is said that whenever the Na'vi face seemingly insurmountable odds a *Toruk Makto* will appear. Neytiri tells Jake that her grandfather's grandfather was the last. As *Toruk Makto* he united the clans "in a time of great sorrow."

Attack leader
Flying on their banshees, the Na'vi warriors join Jake, the new *Toruk Makto*, as he leads them into battle against the human RDA invaders.

MOUNTAIN BANSHEE

Graceful, dangerous, and loyal, the banshee is an integral part of Na'vi life

The *ikran*, or banshee as the RDA named it (for its piercing cry), is a formidable predator. Despite its ferocious appearance, the banshee can be tamed, enabling warriors to embark on spectacular aerial hunts. The Omatikaya clan has a particular connection to the mountain banshee rookery high in the Hallelujah Mountains. Home to the biggest specimens (the best for riding), this rookery is situated on Mons Veritatis, one of the largest of the floating mountains. It is here that the Na'vi come to select—and be selected by—a banshee.

In one of a series of rites of passage called *Iknimaya*, young Omatikaya warriors climb to the rookery and bond for life with a wild banshee—a dangerous, exhilarating experience. Afterward, bonded mountain banshees nest in the branches of Hometree, close to their chosen rider.

A fierce friend
Bonding with a banshee is a two-way process. Each banshee "selects" its potential rider.

Data file

NA'VI NAME: *Ikran*
HABITAT: Mountainous regions, including the Hallelujah Mountains
ANATOMY: Four leathery wings; hollow, carbon-fiber skeleton; large distensible jaw; razor-sharp teeth.
COLORATION: Variable patterns of blues, browns, and greens.
WINGSPAN: Up to 39 ft (12 m)

BONDED FOR LIFE

Bonding with a banshee is a dangerous rite of passage for all Omatikaya warriors. They connect to their banshee by joining their braid-like *kuru* to a similar neural link at the back of the banshee's head. This process is called *tsaheylu*.

Unlike the direhorse, a banshee will only bond with one Na'vi in its lifetime. Banshee and rider spend months together training and learning how to communicate, until each becomes an extension of the other as they soar across the Pandoran skies or weave through the rainforest canopy, hunting on behalf of the clan.

Ready for flight
Seasoned Omatikaya rider Neytiri approaches her mount, ready to take to the skies, while as-yet-unbonded avatar Jake Sully looks on warily.

Perilous journey
Omatikaya clan warriors traverse massive root "highways" through the Hallelujah Mountains to reach the rookery where they hope to bond with their *ikran*.

A WARRIOR'S FIRST HUNT

A successful *Iknimaya* rite of passage not only brings a would-be Na'vi warrior their own mountain banshee, it also seals their status as a full-fledged hunter of the Omatikaya clan. The new hunter is permitted to join other clan hunters in a thrilling sturmbeest hunt.

AERIAL CREATURES

Pandora's skies are filled with wildlife that is amazing, beautiful, and sometimes deadly

One of the first remarkable things RDA xenozoologists note when observing Pandoran aerial lifeforms soaring across the sky, or flapping, buzzing, and humming through the rainforests, is that these incredible creatures have not one, but two, full sets of wings.

The scientists subsequently discover that giant predators such as the mountain banshee (*ikran*) and great leonopteryx (*toruk*) are revered by the Na'vi and feature prominently in their daily lives, lore, and history. The shimmyfly, a delicate butterfly-like insect, is valued by the Na'vi for other reasons: Its iridescent wings, when molted, are used for decoration and jewelry.

By contrast, the fearsome-looking stingbat and the hellfire wasp are best avoided. An angry swarm of hellfire wasps can potentially kill a human being with their stings.

Ikran on the wing
The mountain banshee is a stalwart companion of the Na'vi, whose hunters form lasting bonds with these creatures.

Tetrapteron
Found in flocks mainly in wetlands and on lakes, this four-winged, flamingo-like creature has a twin tail, which assists balance as it hunts for fish. While many predators on Pandora nurture their young, none takes more care of its offspring than the tetrapteron.

Size chart

Docile and beautiful or terrifying and monstrous, the aerial fauna of Pandora comes in many shapes and sizes and with a wide range of wingspans.

Shimmyfly
Wingspan: Up to 1 ft 4 in
(0.4 m)

Tetrapteron
Wingspan: Up to 5 ft
(1.5 m)

Stingbat
Wingspan: Up to 10 ft (3.3 m)

Mountain banshee
Wingspan: Up to 39 ft (12 m)

Great leonopteryx
Wingspan: Up to 102 ft
(31 m)

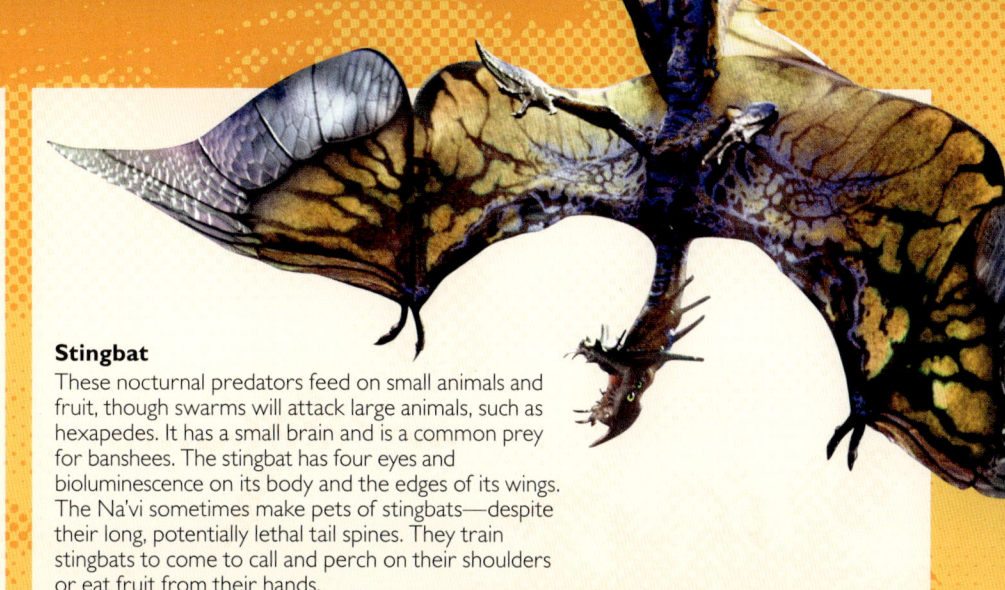

Stingbat
These nocturnal predators feed on small animals and fruit, though swarms will attack large animals, such as hexapedes. It has a small brain and is a common prey for banshees. The stingbat has four eyes and bioluminescence on its body and the edges of its wings. The Na'vi sometimes make pets of stingbats—despite their long, potentially lethal tail spines. They train stingbats to come to call and perch on their shoulders or eat fruit from their hands.

Shimmyfly
These beautiful insects inhabit fields of flowers in the Mo'ara Valley, a neighboring region of the Omatikaya-inhabited rainforest. Apart from their eight wings and large size, their anatomy, life cycle, and behavior are similar to those of butterflies on Earth. Shimmyfly caterpillars feed on leaves; adult shimmyflies feed on nectar from flowers.

Hellfire wasp
With a wingspan of some 11 in (28 cm), and bioluminescence on their body and wings (right), hellfire wasps are easy to spot day or night. Unfortunately, they are not so easy to avoid. If disturbed or threatened they usually attack, and have an agonizing sting. When at rest, hellfire wasps often cluster together in the form of a flower, an effective camouflage from predators.

Nightwraith

The nightwraith is a large, flying creature that is ridden by the leader of the Mangkwan clan, or Ash people. All other Ash warriors ride *ikran* (mountain banshees).

Shroud

In the Clouded Forest, the *loiyokx*, or shroud, is a flying insect whose short life is dedicated to the survival of its eggs, which hatch on the freshly dead body of a larger creature. The shroud covers its eggs with an umbrella-like shield (far right).

Medusoid
Living in the skies of Pandora, medusoids are 910 ft (277 m) tall and generate hydrogen gas. The Tlalim clan (see pp. 110–11) use medusoids to hold aloft their airships, which are then pulled by flying creatures called windrays.

Kinglor
Native to the Kinglor Forest of the Western Frontier, this moth-like insect is 12 in (30 cm) long. It is emblematic of the Aranahe clan and intrinsically linked to its culture.

Stormglider
With an average wingspan of 125 ft (38 m), the *slotsyal*, or stormglider, rides the updraft winds at great heights then swoops down to attack prey, which it stings with its poisonous barbed tail.

Kite manta
In mountainous areas of the Western Frontier's Clouded Forest, the *syo'tsway*, or kite manta, uses its large wings—made from thin, translucent skin—to cruise through the air. It feeds on insects and microorganisms.

AQUATIC ANIMALS

Some of Pandora's strangest and most beautiful creatures inhabit the moon's watery places

Pandora has an incredibly rich ecosystem of aquatic animals. Some, like the turtapede, are gentle giants, similar to Earth's turtles; others, like the fearsome, whale-like nalutsa and the voracious dinicthoid, are deadly predators.

Human xenomarine biologists are well aware that they still have much to discover and understand about the incredible variety of lifeforms that dwell in the depths of Pandora's many lakes, rivers, and oceans.

Nalutsa
Like orca whales on Earth, this six-gilled, 131-ft- (40-m-) long ocean behemoth can be seen leaping out of offshore waters as it hunts its prey. Its cousin, the akula, is even larger.

Sagittaria
These 4 ft (1.2 m) nautilus-like creatures are a combination of mollusk, octopus, squid, and mudskipper. The Na'vi make shields, arrowheads, knives, and beads from Sagittaria shells.

Anemonoid
The rivers and streams of the Pandoran rainforest are replete with starbursts of anemonoids, some up to 3 ft 3 in (1 m) in diameter. They glow and gently sway at the bottom of relatively calm waters, devouring fish and other wildlife that pass within range.

Turtapede
The turtapede can be found lazily swimming through freshwater lakes and rivers, but has also adapted to saltwater oceans. Turtapedes have armored bodies and multiple fins. The dorsal fin increases in size with age, with the armored plates surrounding it falling off and regrowing to fit the increasing appendage. A full-grown turtapede is approximately 16 to 20 ft (5 to 6 m) from snout to tail and 13 ft (4 m) tall.

Dinicthoid
The dinicthoid lurks in Pandora's lakes and lowland waters waiting to strike. This ferocious predator uses its two large, beak-shaped teeth to snare its food. Dinicthoids have a varied diet, which includes plant life and fish of all sizes. A school of these creatures could even bring down a small sturmbeest if one were to wade far enough into a dinicthoid-populated watering hole. An adult dinicthoid can grow up to 10 ft (3 m) in length and swims by flexing its supple, muscular sides.

Elder adult male (bioluminescent)

Juvenile male

Reef tick
This large, 2 ft (0.6 m) insect has a symbiotic relationship with Sagittaria, feeding off scraps that the cephalopods leave behind.

Skimwing

Skimwings, or *tsurak* (in Na'vi), are large, powerful flying fish. They can launch themselves out of the water, propelling themselves with their long tails, which remain in contact with the surface. Reef clans ride *tsurak* on hunts and into battles.

Gill mantle

This invertebrate consists of a small body (with a mouth, brain, and vital organs) and several pairs of translucent fins. Reef Na'vi can attach their *kuru* (neural whip) to the creature and share its oxygen when swimming underwater.

REEF FISH

Coral reefs are home to countless species of fish. For marine Na'vi, fish are valuable food sources and frequently appear in artworks and stories.

Hammerbrow fish
These small, colorful fish live in schools of up to a dozen. They use a pair of sensitive head extensions to detect the presence of would-be predators.

Feathertail fish
This fish's long tail fin allows it to "sprint" for a short time to escape predators. Its two pairs of eyes have enhanced spectral range.

Pincer fish
The small, predatory pincer fish uses its two head tusks to catch prey and battle other pincer fish in jousting matches.

Glider fin
Found in shallow waters in huge schools, the glider fin is a forage, or prey, fish, eaten in large numbers by larger fish, marine birds, and other Pandoran ocean fauna.

Flat skate fish
The vibrantly colored flat skate fish is a fast swimmer, propelled in a kicking motion by its split tail fin. It is considered a delicacy by reef clans.

Ilu
Intelligent and fast, *ilu* inhale air through two nostrils on their head and exhale through multiple spiracles (exhaust ports) along the neck. Easily domesticated, *ilu* are ridden by marine Na'vi, who connect with them via their *kuru*.

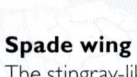

Spade wing
The stingray-like spade wing travels both in groups and alone. The two large forefins that extend from the front of its head are used to funnel prey into its mouth.

Squid lantern
Bioluminescent Pandoran squid lanterns gather in large schools containing hundreds of individuals.

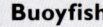

Syringil
This scavenger fish attaches its sucker-like mouth to surfaces and feeds on algae. Its strong grip can withstand ocean currents.

Buoyfish
With a sectioned carapace across its body, this fish is adapted for flexible movement that offers defense against predators.

Starbeak
Found in Pandoran reefs, the Starbeak has stripy spines that run along its back, making it look larger than it really is. It has two "horns" and a sharp barb on its head.

Rockbeak fish
Schools of a dozen or so individuals of this fish feed on aquatic plants and sea snails, using their sturdy beaks to crush hard shells or tear apart tough plants.

Moonfish
The river-dwelling moonfish migrates great distances in search of food and has strong jaws that can clamp down and crack the shells of crustaceans.

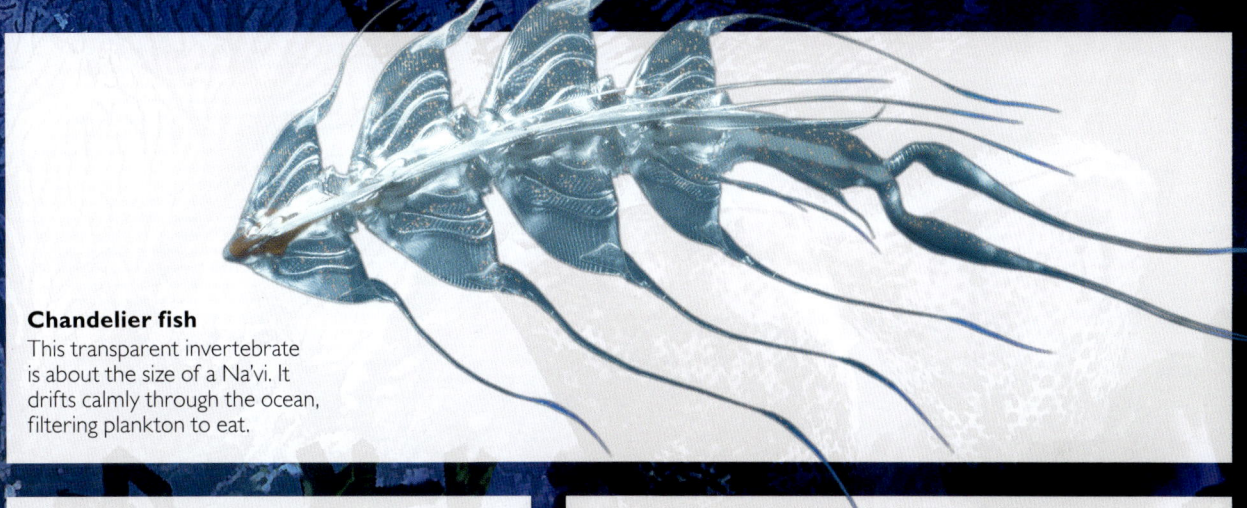

Chandelier fish
This transparent invertebrate is about the size of a Na'vi. It drifts calmly through the ocean, filtering plankton to eat.

Mudcrawler
This fish-like creature slithers across Pandoran riverbeds and can haul itself out of the water to prey on small animals.

Octofin fish
Found in rivers across the Western Frontier, this fish uses its eight lateral fins to propel itself through strong currents with impressive power and agility.

Akula
Called a *pxazang* by the Na'vi, this carnivorous fish possesses three jaws that open in a triangular pattern like a blooming flower.

MOUNTED WARRIOR

Although difficult to tame, skimwings can provide a powerful and fast mount for experienced, strong riders like Jake Sully. During the second RDA invasion of Pandora, Metkayina and Omatikaya warriors ride these awesome flying fish into battle.

Underwater sea life
Coral reefs are one of Pandora's most successful habitats, evolving over millions of years.

CORAL AND ANEMONES

Colonies of marine animals that form and live on reefs

Pandora's tropical seafloors are a habitat for soft and stony dendritic corals, fan corals, and brain corals. These marine animals form colonies and build complex reef structures that can be large enough to protect islands and coastlines from powerful waves and sea-level rises. Pandora's corals filter particles and contaminants from the water, helping to keep the ocean clean.

The reef supports a symbiotic relationship between the various corals and species of anemones, flora, and algae. The reef's health is exhibited by the variety of anemone and coral shapes, sizes, and colors, and by the abundant biodiversity, which scientists believe to be unparalleled in any known ecosystem in the universe.

Daisy anemone
The daisy anemone captures fish with its powerful tentacles. Then it injects paralyzing venom into the prey before digesting it.

Fantail coral
This species anchors itself to rock or hard substrate by its base and uses the stinging tentacle within its central, circular "mouth" to catch zooplankton.

Starry doughnut coral
This large polyp stony (LPS) coral has a hard, ring-shaped exoskeleton with large polyps that collect nutrients from the water around them.

Nom's delight coral
This disk-shaped coral with large polyps on top is free-living: unattached and mobile, it is moved by wave action and fish grazing.

TULKUN

A race of large, highly intelligent marine animals that share an interspecies kinship with the Na'vi

Tulkun have an intellect and cultural development equal to the Na'vi. Like Na'vi, they possess names and rich family histories, as well as sophisticated music and poetry. Eons ago, their social groups warred among themselves, but have since turned away from violence and are sworn to a life of absolute pacifism. In this, they are aided by their anatomy: thick armor plating shields them from natural aggressors without the need for retaliation. Some Na'vi clans, such as the reef-dwelling Metkayina, are sacred and ancient partners with the *tulkun*. Clan members pair for life with a sibling *tulkun*, and the two species share rituals and live together in harmony.

Since the arrival of the RDA, *tulkun* numbers have been under threat as a result of the discovery of *amrita*, a naturally occurring substance found in the *tulkun*'s brain that has the power to halt human aging. *Tulkun* are hunted and killed, and *amrita* is extracted using a specialized drill.

Colorful eyes
Tulkun have four eyes, two on each side of the head. Their unique eye patterns can distinguish individuals.

Sense organs
Like all higher lifeforms on Pandora, *tulkun* possess a neural whip, or *kuru*, which carries "data" in the form of neural signals and provides oxygen and nutrients. Located inside the tulkun's mouth, the *kuru* helps sustain newborns. In addition, sensor whips, used for sensing currents and temperature, trail from beneath the mouth.

Data file

NA'VI NAME: *Tulkun*
HABITAT: Oceans and seas
ANATOMY: Six fins; four eyes; echolocation crests on head.
LENGTH: 65.5–263 ft (20–80 m)
SPEED: 22 knots (25 mph/40 kph)

Agile young
Calves are smaller than adults but, even at a few months old, can swim almost as fast as mature *tulkun*.

MARINE MARVELS

Tulkun are warm-blooded air-breathers, like whales were on Earth. (At the time of the RDA's attempted colonization of Pandora, whales have become extinct.) They live in groupings called pods and feed on shrimp-like creatures and small fish. The large, often brightly colored sensor crests that grow from an adult *tulkun*'s head are lined with sensor pits for echolocation, which give the creatures their enhanced sense of hearing.

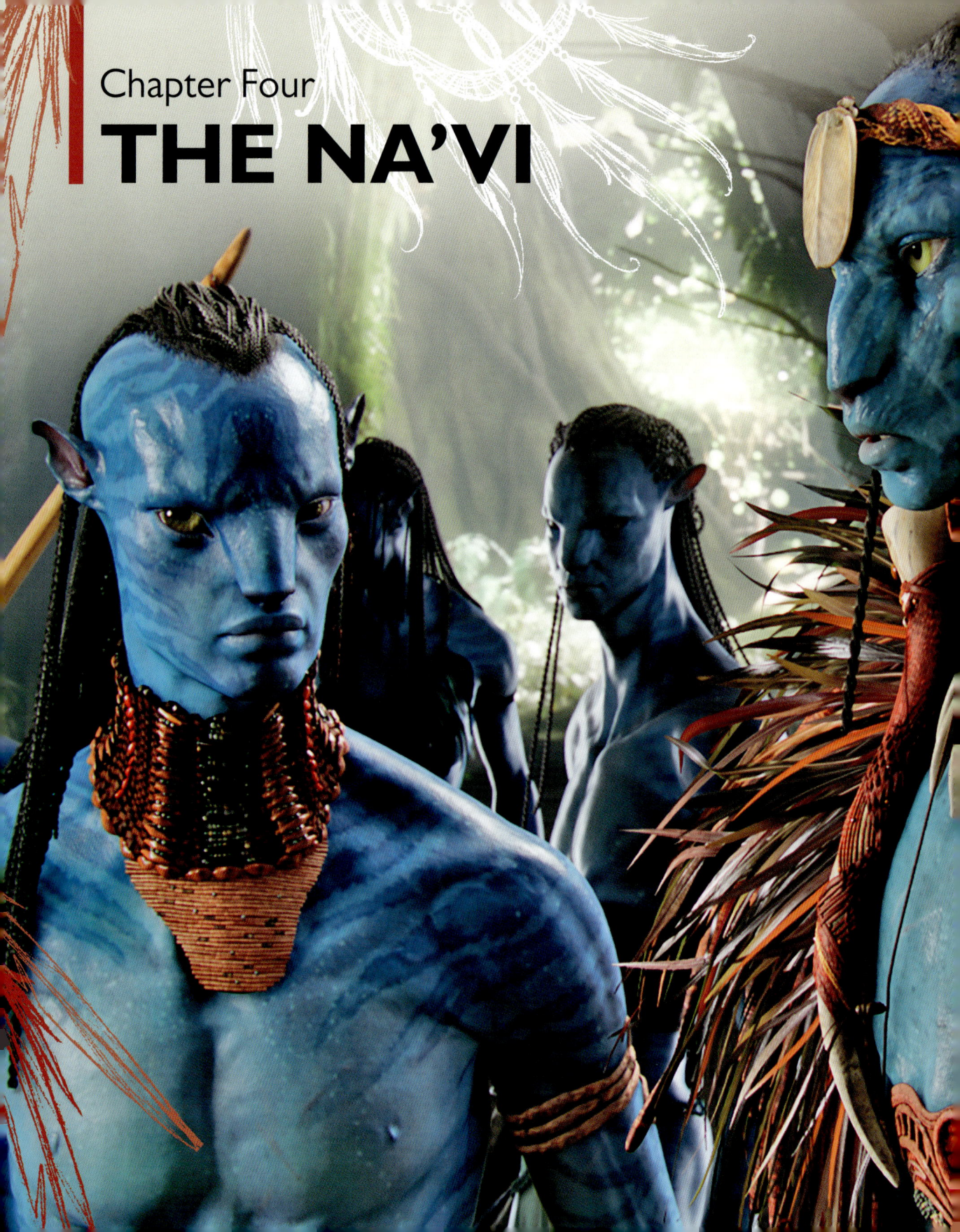

Chapter Four
THE NA'VI

Data file

NA'VI NAME: *Na'vi* or "The People"
ANATOMY: Na'vi vary in size by region and genetic history.
MAX. HEIGHT: 12 ft 10 in (3.9 m)
MAX. WEIGHT: 639 lbs (290 kg)

Na'vi teeth
Na'vi incisor teeth are long and pointed. When angry, the Navi hiss and bare their teeth, giving them a frightening, tiger-like appearance.

Feline ears
Na'vi ears can swivel like a cat's to pick up sounds. The ears' position indicates emotion. When a Na'vi is angry, their ears lie flat.

NA'VI PHYSIOLOGY

The anatomy of Pandora's indigenous inhabitants has similarities, but also crucial differences, to that of humans

In many respects the Na'vi body is human-like, but taller, leaner, stronger, and more slender. The waist is narrow and elongated. The shoulders are wide, creating a V-shaped upper back. The body is slimmer than a human's and is characterized by an elongated neck and long limbs. Na'vi musculature is sharply defined; their physical strength, agility, dexterity, and athleticism is roughly four times greater than that of a human being in peak physical condition.

This means Na'vi are capable of scaling trees or rocks with ease, using their strong fingers and toes to gain purchase. Their speed, agility, and endurance over long distances enables them to keep pace with the animals they hunt. They also possess an uncanny sense of balance and ability to judge distances, enabling them to swing, run, and jump through the rainforest tree canopy. In the unlikely event of a fall, Na'vi usually suffer little harm. Na'vi bones are much tougher than those of a human, being reinforced with a type of naturally occurring carbon fiber.

Distinctive hands
Na'vi have three fingers and a thumb on each hand. This is a key difference from RDA avatars (see pp. 178–79), which have four fingers and a thumb, like a human being.

Feet first
The Na'vi have four toes on each foot; they use their powerful big toes to grip with.

Night vision
Na'vi eyes are adapted for nocturnal hunting and are four times the size of human eyes.

Skin stripes
Pigment patterns vary widely, but are generally bands and stripes of darker blues on a field of lighter blue and cyan tones.

Tail telling
All Na'vi have long, prehensile tails for gripping and balance. Like their ears, their tails communicate emotions.

CONNECTING WITH THE WORLD

At first glance, a human might think that the Na'vi queue, or *kuru*, is simply a long hair braid. However, this braid is a sheath for a "neural whip"—an extension of the Na'vi's nervous system. At its end are neural tendrils that can link to similar connections on animals and plants. This connection enables the Na'vi to command animals such as the direhorse and banshee, and, on rare occasions, even predators like the *toruk* and thanator. More importantly, it allows the Na'vi to access the neural network that envelops the entire moon, and thus the collective wisdom of all Pandoran life. From birth, every Na'vi has their hair painstakingly braided over their neural whip to protect it from harm.

It is difficult to overstate the importance of the *kuru* to the spiritual and physical wellbeing of the Na'vi. The *kuru* allows a Na'vi to connect to racial memories and their ancestors and it is the interface to *Eywa* that pervades all Pandora's biomes.

A bond for life
Neytiri uses her *kuru* to bond with her banshee Seze—a neural connection that the Na'vi call *tsaheylu*.

Bioluminescent patterns
Every Na'vi possesses facial and body pigmentation patterns that take on a phosphorescent glow in darkness. These bioluminescent markings can appear in a varied color palette to indicate mood and emotion.

75

NA'VI SOCIETY

Founded on powerful universal beliefs, Na'vi society and culture is steeped in tradition

Outside of Earth, the Na'vi are the only known species with human-like intelligence; however, their society has developed very differently. Their vibrant and complex culture is based on profound spiritual connections to their world and its natural order, to one another, and to the deity they call *Eywa*. Strict codes govern the Na'vi's actions and keep them pure in the eyes of *Eywa*.

All Na'vi practice the Three Laws of *Eywa*:

You shall not use the metals of the ground.
You shall not carry burdens upon the turning wheel.
You shall not set stone upon stone.

Why or when *Eywa* decreed these laws is lost in the mists of time, but seems to predate even the legendary Time of First Songs. These laws have given rise to a hunter-gatherer society that has not developed into the vast cities and extensive technology seen on Earth.

There are many clans spread across Pandora's diverse environments, from rainforests to deserts, icy tundras, and tropical reefs. Each culture is shaped by its surroundings and has its own rich history, art, music, and mode of dress. This diversity is celebrated, but the Na'vi Way still stands resolutely at the center of their shared experience.

Human interference on Pandora creates a clash of two very different civilizations. The humans (whom the Na'vi call the "Sky People") break all of *Eywa*'s sacred laws.

Low-impact lifestyle
The Na'vi only hunt and gather from nature what they need to live on and to sustain the clan. There is never any waste or unnecessary damage to nature.

A sense of community

For the Na'vi, foraging, hunting, and child-rearing are not roles determined by gender. Each task is valued by the community and shared with the next generation.

SONGCORDS

The songcord is an important part of Na'vi culture. Every individual creates their own songcord as they go through life. When an individual has a milestone experience, such as a betrothal, wedding, battle, hunt, or loss of a friend or family member, they select a polished or water-smoothed stone, shell, crystal, or other natural item to represent that moment in their life's song. This acts as a tactile, mnemonic guide for the singing of their life story.

The song itself follows ancient forms, including traditional rules for word selection, melody, and rhythm. But only the individual and those closest to them know the significance of each bead.

The older a Na'vi gets, the longer their songcord becomes, as they accumulate important events and moments in their lives. When they die, their songcord is sung by those who loved them most, as a form of mourning and remembrance. The songcord is the center of identity and storytelling for individuals, families, and for clan history.

Cycle of life
A child with their whole life ahead is highly valued by the Na'vi. The events that will one day feature on their songcords (marriages, parenthood, battles) may also impact the survival of the clan and peace between clans.

HUNTING TO LIVE

Hunting for food is as vital to the Na'vi way of life as their connection to *Eywa*

Although the Na'vi have great respect for all of Pandora's plants and wildlife, they need to hunt animals for food. When the Na'vi are hunting they do not wear any paint—this is reserved solely for a rite of passage known as the Dream Hunt, or for battle. Clan warriors are not truly warriors in the sense of someone who fights as a career. A warrior is first and foremost a hunter, who is called upon to use their bravery and skill for the clan's defense only in times of need.

"*Sivako!*" ("Rise to the challenge!") is shouted by Na'vi warriors before they begin a hunt, spring from a rocky outcrop onto their *ikrans*, or leap from the rainforest canopy. This powerful cry compels warriors to be utterly fearless and test themselves to the absolute limit—and beyond.

On the hunt
Na'vi carry as little as possible when hunting. If Neytiri shoots an arrow, she retrieves it before returning to Hometree.

Mighty war bow
Eytukan's war bow, called *Tsko a'eoio*, is of shaped wood. The blue vanes are banshee chin vanes, which assist aerodynamic steering when hunting on banshee-back.

Blades, bows, and more
As well as bows and arrows, the Na'vi have a range of hunting weapons, including spears and knives with blades hewn from teeth and crystal.

NA'VI WEAPONS

The two most common Na'vi weapons are knives and longbows. After a Na'vi youth has ridden a banshee and completed their Dream Hunt ritual, they become an adult and may carve a bow from Hometree wood. These bows are the Na'vi's primary hunting weapon.

Na'vi knives have more than one use. The front-facing edge is razor-sharp. The blade's point is sharp enough to easily penetrate the skin of any animal the Na'vi hunt. The outside edge is blunt and rounded, allowing the knife to be used as a small club.

Dead shot
The Na'vi are superb archers, and rarely miss their target. Their arrows are tipped with a toxin that results in a quick kill.

OCEAN LIFE

Fishing and hunting at sea require specialist vessels and tools

For Na'vi sea cultures such as the Metkayina, life is tied to the rhythms and wildlife of their marine habitats. Fish and other sea creatures are an important food source and fishing is an integral part of their culture.

The Metkayina create beautiful canoes on which every detail is finely hand-worked, from the seashells and other materials that decorate bows to the intricate latticework of ropes that harnesses the outrigger to the hull. The shapes, colors, and signature motifs of Metkayina canoes provide a form of identification to other clans.

Each Metkayina family crafts its own seafaring vessel and maintains it over a lifetime to withstand the rigors of hunting and fishing on the open ocean. They are also used in ocean rituals and ceremonies, when they are adorned with flowers. When the canoe is finally dismantled, pieces of it are added to the songcords of family members, such is the vessel's sentimental value.

Paddle power
This outrigger canoe is 28 ft (8.53 m) long and seats up to four adults. With wooden paddles, it reaches speeds of 12 knots (14 mph/22 kph).

Prized blade
The Metkayina look after their knives with great care, believing that a well-tended knife means a healthy clan. This example has a sea glass blade and a woven handgrip.

Hunting weapons

Metkayina knives are crystalline weapons made from super-hard obsidian sea stone. They can cut through the thickest fronds of seagrass and delicately peel the thinnest layer of skin from a fish.

Serrated knife
The tooth pattern on this blade is modeled after akula teeth. Its handle is woven dyed seagrass.

Filleting knife
With a skimwing jawbone blade and a seagrass cording-wrapped handle, this short knife is used for filleting fish.

Na'vi archer
The Na'vi in the Western Frontiers use heavy bows for a variety of purposes, including hunting and defense against RDA weaponry.

BOW AND SPEAR FISHING

In Pandora's Western Frontier, Na'vi hunters catch fish in rivers and lakes using bows and spears. Fishers stand on riverbanks overlooking calm, deep waters and patiently look for "white spots," or small areas of disturbance where the water surface is broken by white foam, indicating the presence of gathering fish. The most experienced hunters know to wait until several white spots combine into a single spot—the most concentrated area of fish for a strike.

Hunting knife
This knife, with its blade of aquamarine sea crystal, fits into a woven seagrass sheath.

CEREMONIES AND RITES

From birth to death, Na'vi lives are dedicated to their role in *Eywa*'s great system

Na'vi clans average 300 members. Populations remain constant because each clan's needs tend to be perfectly balanced with its environment. For every individual who dies, another is born. *Eywa*, the Na'vi believe, provides for all her children, who in turn provide for their clan and ultimately, *Eywa* herself. Each Na'vi individual is born with an innate desire and ability to fulfill a specific role needed for the clan's continued survival. The spiritual energy of the dead influences the natural inclinations of each new child so that the clan is constantly replenished.

The Na'vi embrace death as the agent of change and growth, within both communities and the environment. *Eywa* teaches that death allows progress, as it creates new life that can adapt to a changing world. What humans call evolution, the Na'vi call becoming. Everything is on the path to becoming something else, as *Eywa* commands. This belief is reflected in the Na'vi's pragmatic but respectful attitude to hunting animals.

Na'vi funeral practices vary from clan to clan. For example, the Omatikaya ceremony includes burial among tree roots—a natural resting place for one who has lived their life in the rainforest. The clan honors the dead (and *Eywa*) with singing and chanting. The placing of a seed from the Tree of Souls with the corpse reflects a wish for the soul to return to *Eywa*. The coast-dwelling Tayrangi choose to lay their dead in cliff nooks overlooking the waves. The bodies are consumed by small banshees, who, in turn, are fed upon by the clan's larger mounts. In this way, Eywa's cyclical system of life is once again honored.

The Prayer of the Dead
After a Na'vi makes a kill, they say a prayer over the deceased animal to honor the contribution it has made to *Eywa*:
"I see you Brother, and thank you.
Your spirit goes with Eywa,
Your body stays behind,
To become part of the People."

A Na'vi funeral
When an Omatikaya clan member dies, a hole is dug near the base of Hometree. Friends and family line the hole with flowers.

Calf communion
At the calf communion, Reef Na'vi such as the Metkayina join their spiritual siblings, the *tulkun*, in connecting their newborn children to *Eywa* in a ritual that is sacred to both species.

THE DREAM HUNT

To become a full adult clan member, a Na'vi must complete the *uniltaron*, or Dream Hunt. This is a highly spiritual ceremony—both an individual journey and communal event. The initiate is taken to a holy place accompanied by the clan leaders. Other members gather to give their support.

The leaders administer two psychoactive venoms to the initiate. The *tsahìk* (spiritual leader) provides a glowing worm from Hometree, and the *olo'eyktan* (clan leader) brings an arachnoid. The venoms of both creatures intermingle in the initiate's body, causing great pain and even bringing the initiate close to death. While their body suffers, however, the initiate enters a heightened dream state.

If the initiate survives this traumatic experience, they recount the details of their vision—believed to contain prophetic wisdom from *Eywa*—to the clan leaders. As part of their rebirth as an adult, their vision is then re-enacted by the community in a festival that involves feasting and dancing.

Preparation for the Dream Hunt
Na'vi are painted with ceremonial markings before they embark on the final step of the warrior's journey, the *uniltaron*.

OCEANIC PRACTICES

Each year, on a certain date, hundreds of tulkun and their calves approach the Metkayina village. At the hallowed Cove of the Ancestors, all the new calves born within the last year are brought to the Spirit Tree for their first connection to *Eywa*.

NA'VI LANGUAGE

A common tongue that has remained constant over thousands of years of storytelling

No evidence of a written Na'vi language has ever been found. However, a shared language is spoken by the many Na'vi cultures across Pandora—some thousands of separate communities, clans, and nomadic groups. Each region has its own dialects, but all are unmistakably variants of a common root. Human xenoanthropologists and xenolinguists have proposed many theories for the consistency of this language, despite the wide distribution of population on Pandora. Explanations include specific aspects of Na'vi brain structure and memory, as well as the early domestication of flying creatures, enabling long-range travel and facilitating communication between clans.

Another theory for the uniformity of their language is the Na'vi's oral culture, specifically the use of ceremonial singing to communicate stories through the generations. Weaving, carving, and cave painting also play important roles in recording Na'vi history.

Sign language
The Metkayina use sign language to communicate underwater with each other and with animals such as *tulkun*.

NEW WAYS OF SEEING

The Na'vi perception of space, time, and the unity of all things results in the concept of "seeing"—an idea human visitors to Pandora find hard to grasp. To "see" is to remind oneself to let go of past experiences, particularly negative ones, and perceive new stimuli as if encountering them for the first time. When one learns to "see," pain and suffering are easier to bear, answers to burning questions reveal themselves, and fate guides the seer to fulfill their destiny.

When Na'vi encounter or greet one another, they gesture with their hand from their forehead, extending one hand down toward the other. They also marry this gesture with the phrase "*Oel ngati kameie*" ("I see you.") To the Na'vi, this not only represents the literal meaning of seeing the other person in front of them, but also a spiritual seeing. They are recognizing, seeing into, and understanding each other.

When one Na'vi asks another to "See me," they are asking the other individual to set aside any preconceived notions they may have.

Unspoken words
The Na'vi also use gestures and sign language to communicate key ideas and messages.

OUTSIDE COMMUNICATION

Sharing a common language, the Na'vi are used to communicating easily with one another, no matter where in their world they travel. The sudden arrival of humans on Pandora was the first time the Na'vi were confronted with the problems of learning a new language. Dr. Grace Augustine (see pp. 180–81) started a school to help Na'vi children learn to speak, read, and write English. Her dreams of building close relationships with the Na'vi were thwarted when the RDA suddenly shut down the school and killed some of the pupils. However, Dr. Augustine's initial opening of communication channels enabled relationships between Na'vi and human avatars to be cautiously rebuilt, with avatar controllers learning the Na'vi language in return.

Quick study
Under the tutelage of Dr. Augustine, Na'vi children proved quick learners of English.

Simple lessons
Neytiri, the Omatikaya's *tsahìk*-in-training, teaches an avatar the Na'vi word *menari*, which means "eyes."

HISTORY OF THE NA'VI

The Na'vi have a long and storied history dating back many thousands of years

The Na'vi are a proud people who place great importance on sharing stories of their ancestors with the next generation. These tales—referred to by the Na'vi as the "First Songs"—are not written down, but form a rich oral history. Scenes from them are depicted in cave paintings and artifacts.

The societies portrayed in the First Songs are fundamentally very similar to the Na'vi clans of today, despite the great passage of time between them. Studies by xenoanthropologists suggest the Na'vi have experienced few evolutionary changes or changes in population numbers for at least 12 million years. This can be explained by Pandora's balanced ecosystem and a lack of external pressures, meaning that there was simply no need for the Na'vi to change their ways. The First Songs the Na'vi teach their children thus remain relevant for generation after generation.

Flying into legend
The exploits of the first rider of the *toruk* are central to the Na'vi story and are often depicted in cave paintings and other crafts.

HEROES OF THE NA'VI

One of the most famous of the Na'vi oral historical stories tells of the adventures of Omatikaya clan members Entu and Ralu, along with Tsyal from the Tawkami clan. These three youngsters set out on a quest to save the Omatikaya Hometree from a prophesied disaster. Entu becomes the first Na'vi to manage to ride the deadly winged *toruk*, gaining the title *Toruk Makto* and saving his people. Generations later, the tale of the *Toruk Makto* is still sung and influences the actions of a new generation of Na'vi.

Living up to legends
Tsu'tey has been inspired by the stories of his ancestors since childhood. During his lifetime, the Na'vi face one of their greatest threats—the Sky People. Tsu'tey knows it is time for his generation to emulate the heroics of those that came before them.

THE COMING OF THE SKY PEOPLE

Thousands of years later, the harmony of Pandora is disrupted by the arrival of humans, whom the Na'vi call "Sky People." The peaceful Na'vi initially try to live side by side with these visitors, even welcoming the "Dreamwalker" avatars human scientists use to explore Pandora. Dr. Grace Augustine sets up a Na'vi school, while The Ambassador Program, or TAP, attempts to instill new values in Na'vi children through reculturation (see pp. 186–87).

Na'vi opposition to the Sky People only begins when the humans of the Resources Development Administration (RDA) disturb the fragile balance of nature by mining unobtanium ore and uprooting swathes of the forest. When Jake Sully—former US Marine, avatar driver, and eventually *Toruk Makto*—turns against the RDA, the Na'vi are victorious and drive the ruthless interlopers from their midst. The Na'vi's victory is impressive, but is only the first of several bitter clashes.

Shaman of Songs
An Omatikaya singer, Shaman of Songs, sings the blessing of *Eywa* to humans who visit the Valley of Mo'ara to learn about and celebrate Pandora's environment.

Forced reeducation
Na'vi children in TAP schools were brutalized in order to break down their sense of cultural identity.

RECONCILIATION

Many generations after the great human and Na'vi conflict ends, another, very different human agency, Alpha Centauri Expeditions (ACE), arrives on Pandora and renovates a former RDA base. With the Na'vi's permission, ACE brings human guests to the Valley of Mo'ara.

Though the aftereffects of conflict and environmental damage are still felt, humans and Na'vi at last move forward as one. Together, they ensure the environment remains as undisturbed as possible. The Na'vi also hope that tourists who experience the unique ecosystems of Pandora will return to Earth and spread the Na'vi's knowledge about the importance of connection with the natural world.

Chapter Five
CLANS OF THE NA'VI

One clan, one voice, one people
The Omatikaya all join hands celebrating one of their clan.

OMATIKAYA CLAN

Peaceful rainforest dwellers, the Omatikaya are the humans' window into the Na'vi way of life

The Omatikaya are an ancient clan that has lived and thrived in the rainforests of Pandora for hundreds of generations. While these fierce hunters proudly protect their jungle homeland, they are also a friendly and deeply spiritual people. Their strong connection to nature is evidenced by the Hometree in which they live. They are at one with the natural world around them, riding direhorses and mountain banshees, carving bows from the branches of Hometree, and creating artifacts from plants, shells, and crystals. They are also noted weavers, recognized for their beautiful textiles and woven structures.

Community is hugely important to the Omatikaya. All the important events in an individual's life are celebrated with a communal gathering involving music, food, and dance.

The Omatikaya have developed close relationships with nearby Na'vi clans. Some clans oppose the Omatikaya's decision to admit humans into their society; however, this distrust largely subsides when certain humans—notably Dr. Grace Augustine and Jake Sully—prove that they can make valuable contributions to Na'vi society. When the RDA launches a blistering attack on the Omatikaya's homeland, other Na'vi clans are quick to come to their aid. Victory is shortlived, however, as the RDA returns to Pandora with new forces and strategies for the colonization of the moon. New alliances between Na'vi clans will become necessary to meet this threat.

The "Blue Flute Clan"
All Na'vi clans place great emphasis on music, none more so than the Omatikaya, who are known as the "Blue Flute Clan."

CLAN OF CRAFTERS

The Omatikaya's ropes, twine, and fabric are made from fibrous plants that grow on the forest floor. Each strand is woven meticulously by hand. The Omatikaya believe that if a job is done correctly it should never need to be done again. With this in mind, the clan will take as long as it takes to perfectly construct a single bow, ax, or spear. All Na'vi clans are weavers; each clan's style varies according to the materials available and their lifestyles.

Mo'at

Mo'at is the matriarch, or *tsahìk*, of the clan. She conducts sacred rituals and interprets the will of *Eywa*. Patient and wise, Mo'at is also a healer, an enforcer of law, and a voice of reason.

OMATIKAYA CLAN MEMBERS

Neytiri and her family are leaders at the heart of the Omatikaya community

The Omatikaya were the first clan to encounter human beings when they arrived on Pandora, and were also the first clan to speak with, negotiate, and engage with the *Tawtute*, or "Sky People" in any meaningful way. Mo'at and Eytukan willingly opened their home and their clan to the Sky People, hoping that each race might learn from the another.

At this time, the head of the clan, or *olo'eyktan*, is Neytiri's father, Eytukan. Calm, even stoic, Eytukan often defers to his *tsahìk* partner Mo'at. In the Omatikaya clan, it is traditional that these two important roles belong to a mated pair. Eytukan and Mo'at's eldest daughter, Sylwanin, was due to become the clan's next *tsahìk*, with her betrothed partner, Tsu'tey, taking her father's position as *olo'eyktan*. When Sylwanin is tragically killed by the RDA, her sister, Neytiri, is next in line to become *tsahìk*.

Eytukan

Eytukan was a warrior chieftain and fierce protector of his people. As *olo'eyktan*, he oversaw the training of young warriors and hunters and provided game to feed his clan. He was killed in battle while attempting to stop the RDA from destroying his clan's ancestral Hometree.

Neytiri

Neytiri embodies many typical Na'vi traits. She has a childlike curiosity, but an animal ferocity when provoked. She is a fierce warrior and incredible tracker. The death of her sister Sylwanin in the school massacre scars Neytiri, making her angrier toward humans. Neytiri was expected to marry Tsu'tey, whom she loves only as a friend, but chose Jake Sully as her mate instead.

A WARRIOR CLAN

One of the strongest warriors of his generation, Tsu'tey embodies the Na'vi Way. Although humans killed his betrothed, Sylwanin, Tsu'tey remains in line to become the clan's leader. After the senseless school massacre, Tsu'tey becomes convinced that humans are not merely fools who do not "see," but a threat to his people's very existence.

At first a bitter rival of Jake Sully, Tsu'tey later becomes his friend and comrade-in-arms. At the Battle of the Hallelujah Mountains, Tsu'tey is mortally wounded and passes the mantle of *olo'eyktan* to Jake. Sully leads until the RDA's return forces him to leave for the safety of the clan.

Tsu'tey leads the way
As part of their training, young warriors bound through the rain forest, following the experienced Tsu'tey.

Sylwanin
The eldest daughter of Eytukan and Mo'at, Sylwanin perished at the hands of RDA military forces. She was chosen to become the clan's next *tsahìk*. Her memories live on as part of the Tree of Voices, and she can appear to her loved ones in spirit form when they are tethered to the tree.

Ageless tales
The Omatikaya are a constant and enduring presence on Pandora. Neytiri's family tells her stories of Ralu and Entu, the first *Toruk Makto*, who lived many thousands of years earlier. Generations later, long after the conflict between humans and Na'vi has ended, Shaman of Songs sings these same songs, and many more, to new travelers to Pandora.

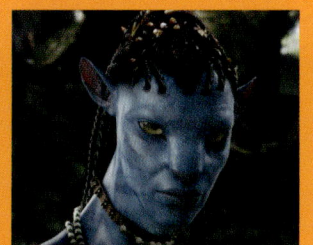

Entu
Thousands of years ago, Entu became the Omatikaya clan's first *Toruk Makto* and saved his homeland.

Ralu
Calm, kindhearted Ralu joined his friend Entu on a legendary journey to tame the flying *toruk*.

Shaman of Songs
Shaman of Songs is an important singer, storyteller, and keeper of clan lore in Na'vi society.

Tarsem
Tarsem accepts the role of *olo'eyktan* from Jake, who deems the young warrior "wise beyond his years."

SULLY FAMILY

The leaders of the Omatikaya become the hunted as the RDA returns with an appetite for vengeance

After his legendary victory at the Battle of the Hallelujah Mountains, the title of *Olo'eyktan* (clan leader) of the Omatikaya passes to Jake Sully, while his betrothed, Neytiri, becomes *tsakarem* (spiritual guide in training). Jake and Neytiri have four children, the first of which, Neteyam, is born soon after the expulsion of the RDA. Their middle son, Lo'ak, is a year younger than Neteyam and a self-perceived underdog who feels like he doesn't live up to his legendary parents and Neteyam's standing in the Omatikaya. Tuktirey (Tuk) is their youngest child; she is an independent and opinionated youngster who has to grow up fast. Neytiri and Jake have also adopted Kiri, who was mysteriously born of Dr. Grace Augustine's dormant avatar. Miles "Spider" Socorro is a human orphan who wishes for nothing more than to be a Na'vi and a member of the Sully family.

Happier days
The Sully family—with Tuktirey still a baby—share a bonding moment in their rainforest home before the return of the RDA.

NEW LEADERSHIP

Jake has led the Omatikaya clan since the deaths of *Olo'eyktan* Eytukan and his successor, Tsu'tey. Responsible for the safety of his people, Jake uses his human background to bring a unique perspective to the role. For example, he has forbidden his clan from finding a new Hometree, knowing it would become a target for the RDA. Jake also attempts to reconcile the Omatikaya and humans. As a result, the Omatikaya build a village near Hell's Gate where the remaining humans on Pandora live.

Jake
Jake now lives permanently as an avatar, though he sometimes feels trapped between two worlds.

ESCAPE TO THE REEF

When the RDA return to Pandora, Jake and Neytiri must make some hard decisions. Believing that RDA forces are hunting him, Jake realizes he must prioritize the security of his people, even over the safety of himself and his family. The Sullys leave the Omatikaya in the relative safety of High Camp, a base hidden within the floating mountains, and start a new life far away with the reef-dwelling Metkayina clan. Here, they will learn the Way of Water and inhabit a completely different world to the rainforest one they have always known.

Tuktirey
The baby of the Sully family, Tuktirey is precocious and adaptable. She becomes fascinated by the world beneath the waves when she meets the Metkayina clan.

Neytiri
Betrothed to Jake and proud mother to her children, Neytiri continues to be a strong warrior. She has also also taken on new responsibilities, being next in line to be *tsahìk*, or spiritual guide, and is learning from her mother, Mo'at, who occupies the role.

Sibling dynamics

Firstborn Neteyam cares greatly for his younger siblings and tries to support them. With their human-like features such as eyebrows and five fingers instead of four, Lo'ak and Kiri have a tendency to feel like outsiders in their own family. They bond with each other and with human child Spider, who Neytiri sometimes believes belongs with his own kind.

Neteyam
Eldest child Neteyam has his father's nobility and is a natural athlete and hunter like his mother.

Lo'ak
Second son Lo'ak is competitive with his "golden child" elder brother and struggles to find his place.

Kiri
Kiri has a strong connection with Eywa and feels a bond with her biological mother, Grace Augustine.

Spider
Spider is a close friend of the family. His parents died at the Battle of the Hallelujah Mountains.

HOMETREE

The Omatikaya's Hometree is a silent sentinel that has stood strong for generations

Over 20,000 years old, Hometree is the spiritual and physical home of the Omatikaya clan. Adult members of the clan gain the right to carve their hunting bows from its wood. Hometree is more than 985 ft (300 m) tall and its diameter is many times that of the largest giant sequoia found on Earth. The interior of Hometree is truly magnificent—a massive, helix-like spiral core boasting multiple levels, where the Na'vi eat, sleep, and enact their rituals and customs. Hometree's circumference is great enough to house hundreds of clan members and it also has a number of radially arrayed natural hollows, supported by columns the size of redwoods.

When human geological surveys identify large deposits of the priceless ore unobtanium beneath Hometree, the sacred tree becomes a prime target for the Resources Development Administration. After its destruction by RDA security forces, the Omatikaya decide to wait before claiming a new Hometree for themselves from the unparalleled richness of Pandora's rainforest.

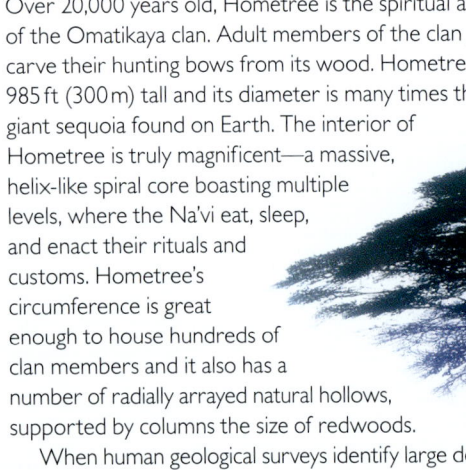

Pillars of the people
Arches, pillars, and spiral root systems have grown and been shaped over thousands of years to create the cathedral-like interior of the Omatikaya's Hometree.

Upper canopy roosts
Banshees roost in the highest tiers of the vast Hometree canopy.

Pleasant dreams
Safe and secure in their massive Hometree, the Omatikaya sleep in hammocks suspended far above the ground.

NATURAL ARCHITECTURE

Inside Hometree are four levels of vaulted spaces. The lowest level, a catacomb among the tree's roots, is reserved for the clan's most sacred rituals. The ground level is a large, open space, while the third level is for communal eating, meetings, and other gatherings. The fourth level is an openwork structure of struts and spokes that is used for sleeping. The Na'vi string their hammocks (or more accurately "cultivate" them, since they are living epiphytes) far above the ground and away from dangerous predators, which at night sometimes prowl among the lower columns.

Burning of Hometree
RDA incendiary rounds engulf the Omitakaya Hometree in flames, forcing the Na'vi to flee along with the forest animals.

INSIDE HOMETREE

The cavernous space surrounding Hometree's immense roots serves many purposes. It is a place where problems can be resolved, strategies discussed, or victories celebrated. Every clan member can attend these assemblies.

HIGH CAMP

A sanctuary for Jake Sully, his people, and the remaining human scientists in the Hallelujah Mountain range

With the return of the Sky People, or RDA, to Pandora, the Omatikaya leader, Jake Sully, and the remaining clan members make the difficult decision to leave the rainforest for their own safety. Their new stronghold, which they call High Camp, is a group of Na'vi *marui* (woven dwellings) located within a concealed cave system inside Mons Veritatis, a large floating mountain in the Hallelujah range. The main grotto is entered not horizontally but vertically by Na'vi riding *ikran* flying up through a large crevasse in the floor. From this defensive base, clan members regularly conduct raids on the RDA infrastructure and supply lines.

The settlement also becomes a field camp for human scientists Max Patel, Norm Spellman, and others, and is equipped with a link shack and a science shack to support avatar as well as Na'vi activity. While High Camp is a last refuge, it also becomes a true home for the remaining humans on Pandora, who live there side by side with the Na'vi. With high technology and indigenous living placed in such close proximity, the tight quarters at High Camp enhance the resistance group's sense of community and combined culture.

TEMPORARY DWELLINGS

In High Camp, families and individuals live in freestanding woven structures called *marui*. These are built from wicker ribs wrapped with robust lashings overlaying a compound curve or triangular frame. The durable structures provide protection from water dripping off the cave ceiling, and can withstand heavy winds. Inside the *marui*, the Na'vi sit together on woven mats next to a fire and sleep in hammocks suspended above the uneven rock surface—away from crawling insects.

Modular structures
Marui range in size from larger ones for families and groups to smaller, individual ones for a single occupant.

Hidden entrance
Jake's flyers can come and go from High Camp undetected by the RDA, provided they exercise the correct formation discipline.

STONY AERIE

When Jake discovered the grotto that would become High Camp hidden deep in the Hallelujah Mountain range, he knew it offered a unique hiding place from the RDA. The cave's natural entrances are tucked beneath the great floating mountain and the chambers are invisible to the RDA's orbital imaging technology. High Camp contains several large community spaces that provide opportunities for leaders to speak and which allow the Omatikaya and their human allies to socialize together.

Field lab
High Camp's biolab houses link beds and an amnio tank that supports Grace Augustine's avatar.

DAILY LIFE

Food preparation and craftsmaking are central to the Omatikaya's way of life

The Omatikaya eat a wide range of foods from their rainforest home, including many types of meat, vegetables, fruit, seeds, and spices. Animals are hunted and consumed only for the good of the clan and in balance with the Pandoran ecosystem. The clan also makes or builds everything necessary for daily life, including baskets, pots, mats, hammocks, and children's toys. Its craftworkers use sustainable materials sourced locally, from wood, minerals, gourds, reeds, and plant leaves to animal hide, bone, and claws.

Inherited abilities
Food preparation and cooking skills are passed down to children, often with songs and rhymes.

Na'vi food

Omatikaya dishes are nutritionally balanced and often served on a leaf plate coated in natural oils and salt or on a decorated board. Some meals are rolled up in an edible leaf and vine wrap called *niktsyey*; these food preparations are usually eaten while hunting and gathering.

Mushroom steak

Octoshroom and fruit salad

Baby squid fruit

Meat feast
This dish contains roasted sturmbeest, hex root, beanpod potato, citrus, and grain.

Root vegetable

Bowl of banana fruit

Containers and receptacles

The Na'vi make simple, functional baskets and carriers, which they often decorate to honor the natural world and to display the maker's pride in their work. Many of these items are used in conjunction with a head or shoulder strap.

Gathering basket
Fruits are collected in large, wide baskets woven from willow-like rods and twine.

Animal-skin water holder

Seedpod basket

Gourd cup

Stirrer

Craftsmaking

All members of the Omatikaya clan practice craftsmaking, with specializations developing over time or through choice. One Na'vi might braid tight bow strings while another stitches leather to form a saddle. Each clan member contributes to the good of the whole, forming a cooperative system and a societal bonding that has sustained the Omatikaya for tens of thousands of years.

Hammocks

Animal toy
Children make models of animals they see in the forest, like this six-legged *yerik*, or hexapede.

Rolled floor mat

METKAYINA CLAN

Oceanic Na'vi who live among the reefs and atolls of Pandora

As one of the Na'vi sea cultures, or "Reef People," the Metkayina dwell in a coastal region distinguished by reefs and atolls. They live in harmony with the ocean and its sustaining fauna, and cultivate a special and personal relationship with the sea. From a young age, they learn how to navigate the waves in canoes. As they grow older, the Metkayina begin to explore the larger and more dangerous waters near the reef's outer seawall. They ride domesticated sea animals called *ilu* and have a unique and spiritual interspecies kinship with gigantic, highly intelligent sea creatures called *tulkun*.

The clan builds its villages among giant mangrove-like trees, and has developed a strong and trusted sense of community. Meals are shared, with everyone contributing food and stories. The Metkayina diet includes much cooked fish, seasoned with herbs and spices that are picked locally or traded with other clans.

The Metkayina have peaceful relations with their neighboring clans, yet are renowned as fierce warriors who will protect their home at any cost.

Meeting of clans
A Metkayina lookout blows a shell horn to alert the clan to the arrival of the Sully family on their *ikran*.

Oceanic inspiration
The Metkayina honor their sea environment in all their constructions, and take inspiration from the sea in everything they do.

Ronal
As well as being *tsahìk*, Ronal hunts, gathers, cooks, and takes part in every aspect of clan life.

METKAYINA CLAN MEMBERS

Tonowari
Despite initial opposition from Ronal, Tonowari offers *uturu* to the Sully family.

Tonowari and Ronal lead their people with dignity and strength, facing down the RDA threat

The Metkayina clan's *olo'eyktan* (leader), Tonowari, oversees his community with a fierce demeanor, strong ideals, and an unerring ability to lead his people through times of challenge. As *tsahìk* (shaman), Ronal, who is married to Tonowari, is responsible for the spiritual needs of the entire clan, and is also an accomplished hunter and warrior, willing to put everything on the line to protect her people. Ronal and Tonowari have two children—Tsireya and Ao'Nung—with a third on the way.

When Jake Sully and Neytiri come to the distant atolls to seek *uturu* (sanctuary), Ronal initially rebuffs them, unwilling to accept the reality of the coming war with the RDA and choosing to look down upon the Sully family. She does not believe that the Sully family—rainforest people—can earn their keep and find a way to live among the seagoing Metkayina.

Waterborne warriors
Tonowari, Ronal, and the Metkayina fighters ride flying fish called skimwings into battle.

DISTINCTIVE FEATURES

The Metkayina have large eyes with a nictitating membrane for perfect underwater vision. Their powerful forearms and lower legs include fin-like structures for faster swimming speeds and their wide tails provide propulsion. Like many reef clans, the Metkayina practice the art of tattooing. Each individual's tattoos are unique, and chronicle their life while also denoting family and rank. Tattoos are considered a gift from both *Eywa* and the clan, and are created with inks from special animals.

Funeral in the water
The Metkayina clan hold a water burial for Neteyam after he is killed by the RDA.

EMPOWERING RITUALS

As *tsahìk*, Ronal leads all ceremonies for the Metkayina clan. At the First Breath ceremony, for example, the entire clan are present for the "water birth" of a Na'vi baby in shallow water. Ronal assists the mother in guiding her newborn as it kicks to the surface to take its first breath, a symbolic transition from water to air. The Metkayina also share this ceremony with any *tulkun* who are gestating. *Tulkun* mothers give birth to their calves alongside the Na'vi, and both newborns will be welcomed by the community.

Ceremonial symbol
The shell necklace that Ronal wears as *tsahìk* contains a small, needlelike knife used for ceremonial purposes.

Young helpers

Tonowari and Ronal's children, Tsireya and Ao'Nung, and their friend, Rotxo, are tasked to guide the Sully family and help these rainforest Na'vi navigate the ways of the Reef People. They help the Sully children learn diving and swimming skills and improve their underwater breath-holding. They also teach them Metkayina sign language, used when swimming underwater.

Ao'Nung
Fifteen-year-old Ao'Nung is respected by others in his community as a skilled diver and hunter.

Tsireya
An advanced swimmer and leader-in-training, thirteen-year-old Tsireya is expected to succeed Ronal as *tsahìk*.

Rotxo
Ao'Nung and Tsireya's confident and daring friend Rotxo likes to go hunting as far out to sea as possible.

METKAYINA VILLAGE

The reef clan's waterside dwellings consist of beautifully and artfully woven structures

Metkayina villages, many of which are thousands of years old, are located on the coast of Pandora's Eastern Sea. The main village, Awa'atlu, where the Sully family make their new home, has small docks for canoes and a centralized pen for *ilu*, large sea creatures that the Metkayina (and other reef clans) use as mounts. Dwellings, known as *marui*, hang between the roots of enormous mangrove trees, with communal areas for gathering, eating, storytelling, and singing. All Metkayina structures are strong enough to withstand Pandoran storms but light enough to leave tree roots unharmed. *Marui* are constantly renewed but seldom replaced. Almost all resources that the Metkayina use for constructing and repairing their *marui*—as well as all the tools they use—are taken from the reef and surrounding ocean, and the island forest. Metkayina clan members are careful only to take from the water exactly what is needed so they do not deplete the ocean of life.

Totem design
The *marui* the Sully family stay in is designed with a welcoming, open shape.

Suspended habitations
Marui are supported by and tensioned on gigantic root systems that grow in twists and turns around the dwellings.

Data file

NA'VI NAME: *Marui*
LOCATION: Mainly coastal (sometimes used as temporary structures in other locations)
CONSTRUCTION: Fabric and wooden frames

HANDCRAFTED HOMES

Marui are built from stripped and woven Pandoran flax and rattan, with transparent fabric membranes that let in light and provide color. Woven walkways, held rigid by tension points anchored to mangrove roots, allow access to other areas. Fish pens made of bamboo are typically suspended from the bottoms of *marui*, above the water surface.

Learning from the sea
When the Sully family start a new life with the Metkayina, they deepen their respect for the oceans.

Grand flotilla
Wind Traders travel in groups for protection. Na'vi outriders on *ikran* provide hunting, scouting, and guard functions.

TLALIM CLAN
A nomadic and trade-driven people that travel across Pandora by air

The Tlalim, commonly known as the Wind Traders, have taken a different path from other Na'vi clans, most of which prioritize hunting and gathering for their livelihood. These sharp and resourceful nomads are traders, constantly on the move, traveling in convoys of gigantic gondolas. They make periodic visits to various Na'vi cultures, setting up a market at each destination—usually a village. The Na'vi do not have a monetary system, so trade is conducted through bartering and the exchange of goods, which include dried meats, exotic fruits and vegetables, tools, textiles, and crystals. Wind Traders also bring stories about other Na'vi people and receive local messages and tales to pass on during their travels. The arrival of the Tlalim is a welcome sight that signals a feast and dancing.

NAVIGATING THE SKIES

The Tlalim sail through the air in elegantly-woven gondolas held aloft by giant jellyfish-like medusoids—living hydrogen gas bags with long tentacles. Gondolas are towed by large, self-propelled animals called windrays, which are tethered to the bows of the gondolas using long ropes. Medusoids and windrays can travel for thousands of miles without needing to rest—long after an *ikran* gives out.

Peylak
The Tlalim's *olo'eyktan* is the brave and wise Peylak, who captains the gondola fleet and manages the crews. He is a believer in the importance of enjoying the good life.

MANGKWAN CLAN

A hostile, aggressive, and warlike people that deny the Na'vi belief in *Eywa*

The Mangkwan are violent raiders who pillage neighboring villages for resources, often bringing death and destruction. Living in the burned-out husk of their destroyed Hometree after eruptions from a nearby volcano, the Mangkwan have turned against *Eywa*, believing she had turned her back on them by not interceding in the volcanic tragedy that destroyed their biome.

As a symbol of their perceived rejection, the Mangkwan cover themselves with white and gray ash adorned with red-and-black paint—hence their alternative name, Ash People—and embrace a conqueror's path, which they believe will ensure their clan's survival and reinforce their control over their environment.

Even before the natural disaster, the Mangkwan had a history of hostility and were avoided and shunned by most Na'vi. Since the volcanic desolation of their clan, they have chosen to separate themselves further as aerial raiders and pirates.

Smoke and fire
Here we see the Mangkwan Clan performing a ceremonial fire dance.

Raiders' base
The Mangkwan village is a stark collection of yurt structures in the center of their Hometree ruins.

EQUIPPED FOR CONFLICT

The Mangkwan's weapons are lethal and crudely made. Knives have jagged blades made of crystal, bone, and metal, while spears, swords, and axes are constructed from bone, petrified wood, and metal. Y-shaped bows, with two upper limbs and one lower limb, are made from trees intentionally cut down to spite *Eywa*. Warriors swing bolas, heavy seedpods, at targets to wrap around their legs, immobilizing them.

Varang
The clan's *tsahik*, Varang, is a ruthless sorceress who witnessed the volcano's devastation as a little girl and is motivated by the apparent rejection of *Eywa*.

OTHER NA'VI CLANS

The Na'vi community comprises many ancient clans, each with its own rich history and culture

Although humans have only really had dealings with the Omatikaya, there are many other Na'vi clans that live and thrive across Pandora. Every Na'vi clan has its own way of life and has made its own special contribution to the complex tapestry of Na'vi culture. Some clans are famed hunters and gatherers, while some are expert artisans. Each clan has a single leader, known as *olo'eyktan* if male and *olo'eykte* if female.

The clans of the Na'vi are generally not aggressive with each other, and have various strategies to resolve conflict. However, they are extremely fierce when provoked. War among clans is not unknown, especially when habitat or territory changes rapidly. This is usually a result of external pressures, such as flooding, rather than deliberate invasion. Na'vi warfare is characterized by fierce fighting. However, custom demands such battles are immediately followed by bargaining, negotiation, and other efforts to bring about peace. Despite their differences, most clans are ultimately brought together by a shared love and respect for Pandora and its guiding deity, *Eywa*.

THE TAYRANGI

The Tayrangi are one of the most prominent clans of the Ikran People—a general term that refers to those clans who ride the *ikran*, or mountain banshee. The Tayrangi live on the edge of a cliff, perched over the tempestuous Eastern Sea. The sea is a source of food for the clan, who have mastered banshee-diving as a form of fishing. Banshee and rider dive into the waves at high speed, submerging for brief periods before returning to the sky. If this dangerous maneuver is not executed properly, the rider could easily be killed.

When called upon by the neighboring Omatikaya clan and *Toruk Makto*, the Tayrangi provide staunch support to their allies. Their honed, aerial hunting tactics give them a considerable advantage against unsuspecting RDA pilots.

Ikeyni
The Tayrangi's *olo'eykte* is named Ikeyni. Her body paint and battle cry rally her people to the Omatikaya cause.

THE TAWKAMI

These gentle, jungle-dwelling Na'vi are natural botanists, chemists, and alchemists. Other clans may see a verdant and beautiful forest, but the Tawkami see a precious collection of ingredients, each with its own special powers and virtues. The Tawkami combine these natural elements to create powerful potions and remedies in recipes that have been refined over many generations. The earliest Na'vi stories tell of a Tawkami youngster named Tsyal. She used one of the clan's most sacred seeds to help the first *Toruk Makto* subdue the ferocious *toruk*.

Seeker and healer
Tawkami clan member Alira likes to explore deep within the jungle, sometimes for weeks at a time.

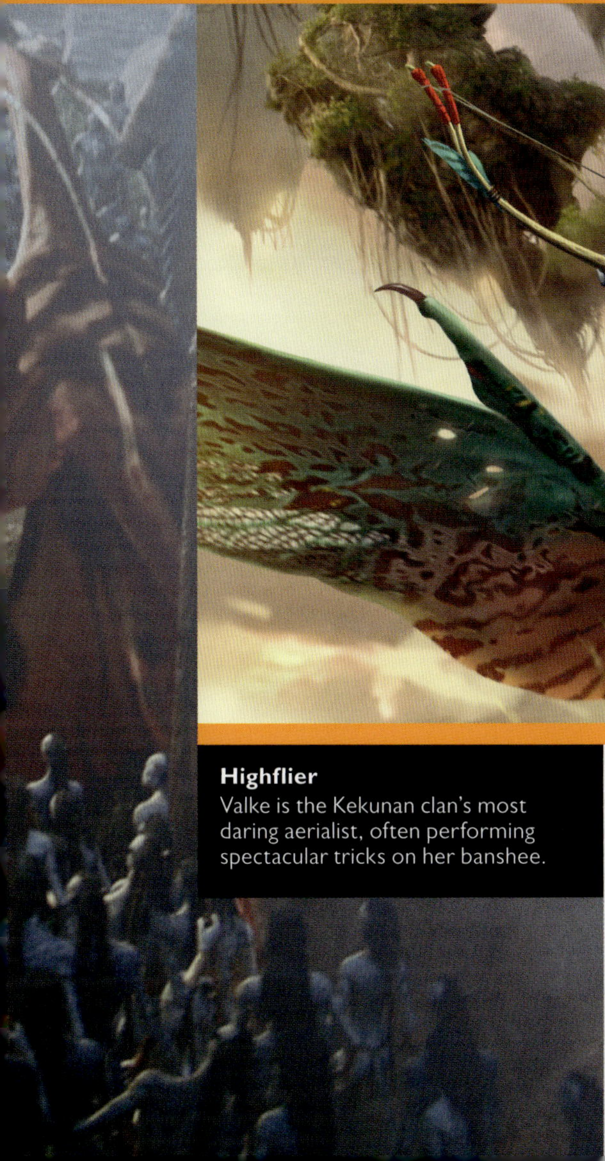

Highflier
Valke is the Kekunan clan's most daring aerialist, often performing spectacular tricks on her banshee.

THE KEKUNAN

This daring Na'vi clan makes its home at the base of sheer and dangerous mountain cliffs. Like the Tayrangi, the Kekunan are masters of banshee flight. Legend even says that the first Na'vi to bond with a banshee was a member of this clan. Kekunan youngsters train for banshee riding at an early age, developing the reflexes and nerve the Kekunan people are famed for. The Kekunan dress in bright, festive colors to show their confidence; riders often select shades that match the vibrant patterns of their banshee mounts.

THE ANURAI

This ancient clan specializes in the wisdom of the night sky. Its members track the movement, and chart the alignments of, stars, planets, and moons. The Anurai are also Pandora's most accomplished artists. Their unparalleled craftwork—musical instruments, visual art, and jewelry—is highly valued across Pandora and even in Earth's black markets.

While some Anurai artisans search the land for perfect materials to turn into works of art, the majority of the clan has settled in a vast, sacred bone sanctuary. Here, they take the ancient bones of animals whose spirits now run with *Eywa* and transform them into beautiful artifacts.

Treasured items
Artisan Ahulang and *Tsahìk* Tiali wear intricately beaded jewelry; such adornments are a defining aspect of Anurai culture.

THE TIPANI

The Tipani are perhaps the fiercest warrior clan of all the Na'vi people. Their hunting prowess is renowned far and wide. They live in more than a dozen small villages scattered throughout the dense jungles of Pandora.

Though all Na'vi are proficient fighters, the Tipani train like no other clan. They raise their children to be warriors from a very young age. When the Tipani hunt, they move without making a sound. This silent hunting style is reflected in the Tipani's otherworldly demeanor. A Tipani rarely speaks, but when one does, it is with careful consideration and often carries considerable weight.

Combat ready
With their trademark armor made from the shells of the cuirass crab, the Tipani clan are always ready for the hunt.

THE OLANGI

Vast, grassy plains are roughly a day's banshee flight away from the Omatikaya's rainforest. This very different topography is home to a group of various horse clans, including the Olangi. More nomadic than most Na'vi, the Olangi follow the migration patterns of the animals they hunt.

Other Na'vi clans ride the direhorse, but the animal is a truly intrinsic part of Olangi culture and the clan's chosen battle mount. The Olangi provide excellent ground support to the Omatikaya during the battle to save the Tree of Souls from destruction by the RDA.

Akwey
The physically imposing *olo'eyktan* of the Olangi Clan, Akwey is a superb rider and a fearless warrior.

KAME'TIRE CLAN

Living in the Clouded Forest of the Western Frontier, the Kame'tire are suspicious of outsiders and prefer to stay hidden, only reluctantly providing support against the RDA. Known for its great healers and herbalists, the clan also practices the dying art of woodshaping. This unique technique involves the gentle molding of wood for use in dwellings, crafts, masks, armor, weaponry, and even prosthetic limbs. The clan's *tsahìk*, Anufi, lives in exile, leaving her advisor, Mokasa, in charge. He controls the clan and keeps the outside world at bay.

Herbal remedies
The Kame'tire are producers of potions: mixtures of herbs and compounds that produce healing effects. They use a modified potion recipe to create smoke bombs.

ZESWA CLAN

The Zeswa are nomads that live in the Western Frontier's Upper Plains. They are led by a forceful warrior, Nesim, whose even fiercer sister Minang serves as clan *tsahìk*. This proud, fearless clan lives in symbiosis with *zakru*, gigantic empathic animals who can sense the presence of danger. The Zeswa are also skilled direhorse riders and are renowned for their warlike competitions and over-the-top celebrations. Boisterous and loving, the Zeswa talk loudly, feel strongly, and play fiercely.

Proud warrior
The Zeswa's *olo'eykte* is the charismatic Nesim. A formidable and determined warrior, she lost her left eye in the fight against the Sky People.

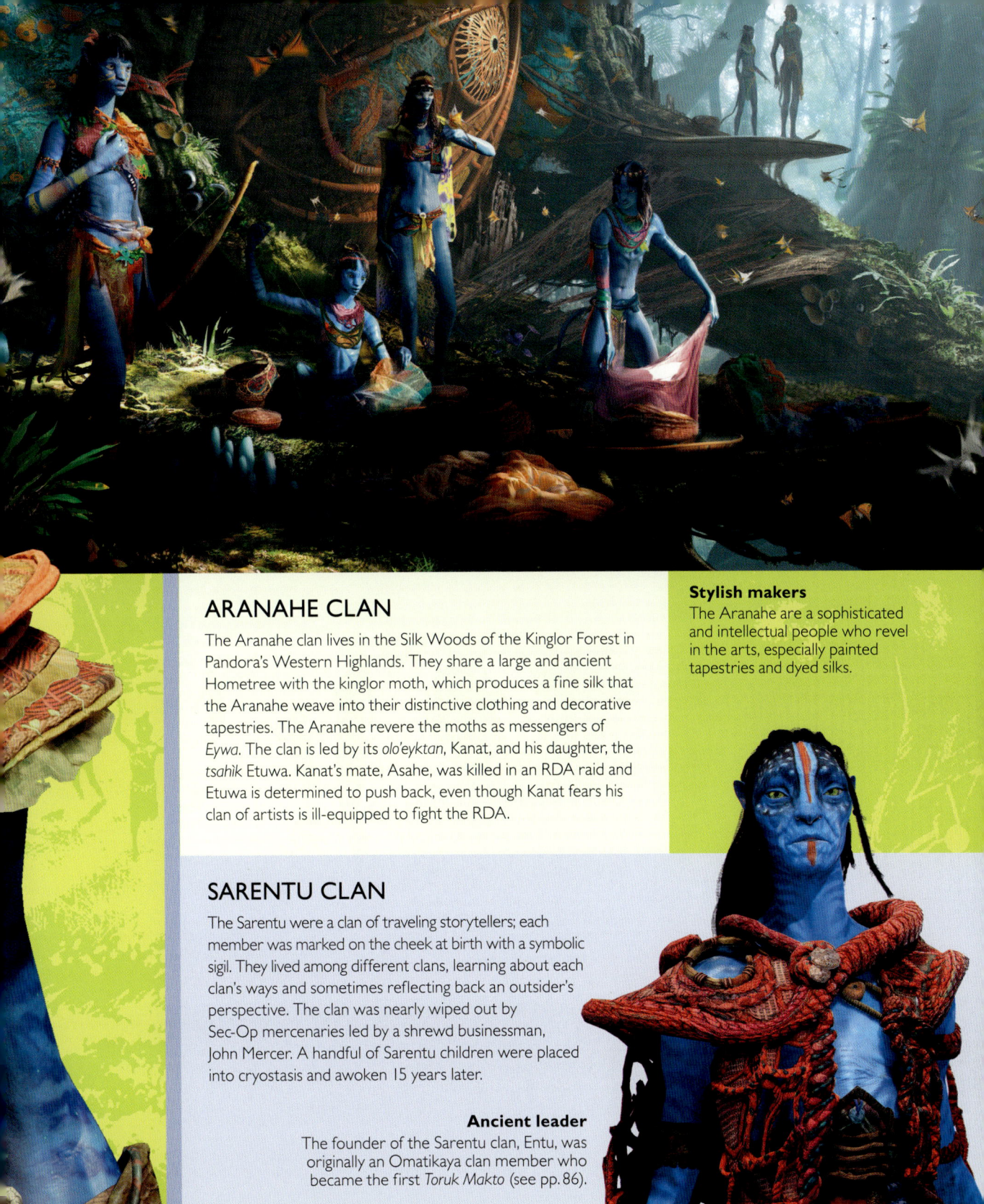

ARANAHE CLAN

The Aranahe clan lives in the Silk Woods of the Kinglor Forest in Pandora's Western Highlands. They share a large and ancient Hometree with the kinglor moth, which produces a fine silk that the Aranahe weave into their distinctive clothing and decorative tapestries. The Aranahe revere the moths as messengers of *Eywa*. The clan is led by its *olo'eyktan*, Kanat, and his daughter, the *tsahìk* Etuwa. Kanat's mate, Asahe, was killed in an RDA raid and Etuwa is determined to push back, even though Kanat fears his clan of artists is ill-equipped to fight the RDA.

Stylish makers
The Aranahe are a sophisticated and intellectual people who revel in the arts, especially painted tapestries and dyed silks.

SARENTU CLAN

The Sarentu were a clan of traveling storytellers; each member was marked on the cheek at birth with a symbolic sigil. They lived among different clans, learning about each clan's ways and sometimes reflecting back an outsider's perspective. The clan was nearly wiped out by Sec-Op mercenaries led by a shrewd businessman, John Mercer. A handful of Sarentu children were placed into cryostasis and awoken 15 years later.

Ancient leader
The founder of the Sarentu clan, Entu, was originally an Omatikaya clan member who became the first *Toruk Makto* (see pp. 86).

119

REY'TANU CLAN

A hundred years ago, the Rey'tanu moved into Pandora's arid Highlands, subduing the powerful beasts that lived there—all except the savage harpetooth. To avoid this dangerous animal, the clan moved to the safety of the Mushroom Rocks, with its oasis and Spirit Tree cavern. The clan relies on agriculture and grazing, and especially its water source, for its survival.

Spiritual leader
Angat is the Hulanta's *tsahìk* and the mate of its *olo'eyktan*, Tiaru.

Saotun
The Rey'tanu's *olo'eyktan*, Saotun, is a descendent of Havang, a legendary figure who sacrificed his life so the clan could stay in the Highlands.

HULANTA CLAN

The Hulanta Clan live in Pandora's Wetlands, a region lined with rivers that form spectacular waterfalls. Experts in pottery and weaving, the clan use swirling patterns in their designs to represent water, which they consider to be sacred. In a rite of passage ceremony, children must cross a river in order to become Hulanta. The clan gather for bonfire celebrations within their Hometree, which is protected from the flames by the humid air of the Wetlands.

Forest hunters
The Hulanta are skilled hunters. They reward good deeds with a Ceremonial Bow, which they craft using branches that have fallen from their sacred Hometree.

TA'UNUI CLAN

The Ta'unui are an oceanic Na'vi clan who live in the same group of atolls on the Eastern Sea as the Metkayina. In 2170, the Ta'unui's village is targeted by Miles Quaritch and a team of Recoms looking for Jake Sully. Frustrated that the clan does not reveal any information about Jake, Quaritch orders his squad to burn down the village, leaving the Na'vi in despair.

Under questioning
Facing Colonel Quaritch, the first instincts of the Ta'unui *olo'eyktan* and *tsahik* are to protect their People and give the human invaders nothing.

TRR'ONG CLAN

Founded by Hawnutu'un, a warrior who lived at the time of Entu, the first *Toruk Makto* (see pp. 86–7), the Trr'ong clan lived near the Omatikaya in the region of the Hallelujah Mountains. The clan suffered heavy losses in the battle against the RDA; most of the few survivors were given refuge by other clans.

Battle survivor
Trr'ong warrior So'lek survived the Battle of the Hallelujah Mountains and traveled to the Western Frontier to continue the fight against the RDA.

Chapter Six
SACRED SITES

NA'VI BELIEFS

The Na'vi's deeply rooted belief system promotes harmony between all living things

Na'vi clans across Pandora share certain key values, such as a deep respect for nature, that stem from their shared belief in a globally distributed consciousness of Pandora called *Eywa*. Also known as the All-Mother or the Great Mother, *Eywa* is the Na'vi's primary deity. The Na'vi also believe that all living things have a spiritual counterpart, or soul. At the end of life, this spirit returns to the consciousness of *Eywa* and is brought back as living matter in an eternal cycle of death and rebirth.

The Na'vi see all aspects of nature as a single connected system to be respected and cared for. However, they revere certain trees and plants as sacred—as places where *Eywa* herself is believed to reside, such as the Tree of Souls. Animals and the Na'vi have free will and are not, strictly speaking, a part of *Eywa*—in the same way a child is not a part of the mother, but does owe life to her.

The Na'vi desire to live in harmony with their world. Their oneness with *Eywa* provides them with a sense of certainty, selfless values, and pure motives. The Na'vi's trusting ways can appear naive to humans, some of whom hope to prey on the Na'vi's perceived innocence. After the first attempted human invasion of Pandora, *Eywa* developed an "immune reaction" of dispatching animals to protect the moon.

Moment of reflection
Neytiri visits the sacred Tree of Souls to commune with *Eywa*.

Forest gathering
The Na'vi look for signs from *Eywa* in the natural world. For example, Neytiri and her mother Mo'at—the Omatikaya clan's *tsahìk*—seek answers to spiritual questions from the *atokirina*—seeds of the Tree of Souls, known by humans as woodsprites.

THE NATURAL AND THE DIVINE

The Na'vi do not view *Eywa* as an all-powerful, world-creating deity. They also do not believe there are other gods, demons, or spirits associated with the non-living forces of the world, such as mountains, rivers, or volcanoes. The Na'vi know that storms, floods, and other natural phenomena are uncontrollable forces. Instead, *Eywa* acts as a defender of life and its balance, who helps, protects, and guides the Na'vi against such life-threatening assaults of nature.

Sacred plant
Na'vi of the Western Frontier's Sarentu clan make a neural link to a giant, flowering plant called a tarsyu, which enables them to commune with the memories of their ancestors within *Eywa*.

EYWA'S MESSENGERS

Atokirina (or woodsprites) are seeds from the Tree of Souls that grows on Pandora. According to the Na'vi, these seeds are very pure and sacred spirits. They are similar in appearance to small, deep-sea jellyfish, but they float on the wind like dandelion seeds. Woodsprites are sacred to the Na'vi and are often seen as the bearers of omens and signs.

Connecting to *Eywa*
Gathering at the base of the Tree of Souls, the Na'vi call to *Eywa*—either to express thanks, make requests for guidance, or perform a healing rite.

THE TREE OF SOULS

The spiritual center for the Na'vi's connection to *Eywa*

Situated in a valley of spectacular stone arches, the "Tree of Souls" (*Vitraya Ramunong* in Na'vi) is a huge, weeping willow-like tree with long, bioluminescent tendrils and a large, semi-exposed root system. The Na'vi believe that the tree is their closest connection to *Eywa*. They also maintain that it enables *Eywa* to interact with the world, and that the tree's jellyfish-like seeds—called *atokirina* (woodsprites)—contain spirits that are in communion with *Eywa*. The Na'vi interpret the seeds' movements as important omens: where the seeds drift, where they settle, and whether they cluster has great significance for them.

RDA operatives also have a keen interest in the sacred site of the Tree of Souls. For them, the presence of the stone arches indicates a major magnetic field and an area rich in precious unobtanium. The area surrounding the Tree of Souls soon becomes one of the busiest, most covetable, and most fought-over sites on Pandora.

The power of the tree
The Tree of Souls' roots are incredibly powerful. A human consciousness has not only been successfully "uploaded" to *Eywa*, but has also been transferred from one body to another. *Eywa* works in mysterious ways.

DIVINE COMMUNION

In times of need, Na'vi clan members sit arm in arm in the shadow of the great Tree of Souls and link their braid-like *kurus* to its exposed roots, forming a neural link. Through this ritual, each of the Na'vi experiences a simultaneous connection to the others—a condition of profound emotional power for them. According to the *tsahìk*, this connection enables clan members to better "see" each other and amplifies any message they may have for *Eywa*. Reflecting the interconnections of *Eywa*'s overall creation, clan connection is the strongest statement of purpose the Na'vi can make. The Tree of Souls is currently the only site on Pandora where clan-wide connection is known to occur.

THE TREE OF VOICES

A wonderful repository of all of the Omatikaya's ancestors' voices, thoughts, and lives

The *Utraya Mokri* or "Tree of Voices" is a great tree containing all the stored memories of the Omatikaya clan in its neural core. It even contains the "memories" of the rainforest's abundance of animals and plants.

All of these memories are stored in the natural neural network that is *Eywa*, the Na'vi's deity, and are accessed through Na'vi prayer and ritual. A Na'vi communes with the Tree of Voices by entwining their braid-like *kuru* with the tree's roots and attuning themselves with what they hope to see, feel, or hear. *Eywa* quickly responds, and the wealth of experience from all those who have previously communed with the Tree of Voices becomes available to the individual for exploration and interpretation.

Forging a link to the past
Prior to any great act, Na'vi will visit the Tree of Voices to entrust their memories to *Eywa*.

Bittersweet contact

The Tree of Voices is like a massive data storage system for the collected memories of departed Na'vi. Some Omatikaya only occasionally link with the tree; others may link on a daily basis, "uploading" their thoughts, memories, hopes, and dreams to *Eywa*. When a family member has died, the others may go to the Tree of Voices, connect their *kuru* and "speak" to the deceased. The dead only know and remember things up to the point of the last time that they linked to *Eywa*, via the tree, before their death. It is a bittersweet communion for many. Although living family members can interact once more with their loved ones, now in the embrace of *Eywa*, the communication is only fleeting and ceases the moment the *kuru* is untethered.

In another world
The bioluminescent glow of the tree and its surroundings evoke wonder and awe in all who visit this sacred place.

Seeking lost love
Na'vi warrior Tsu'tey visits the Tree of Voices to contact his beloved Sylwanin, Neytiri's sister, killed by RDA mercenaries.

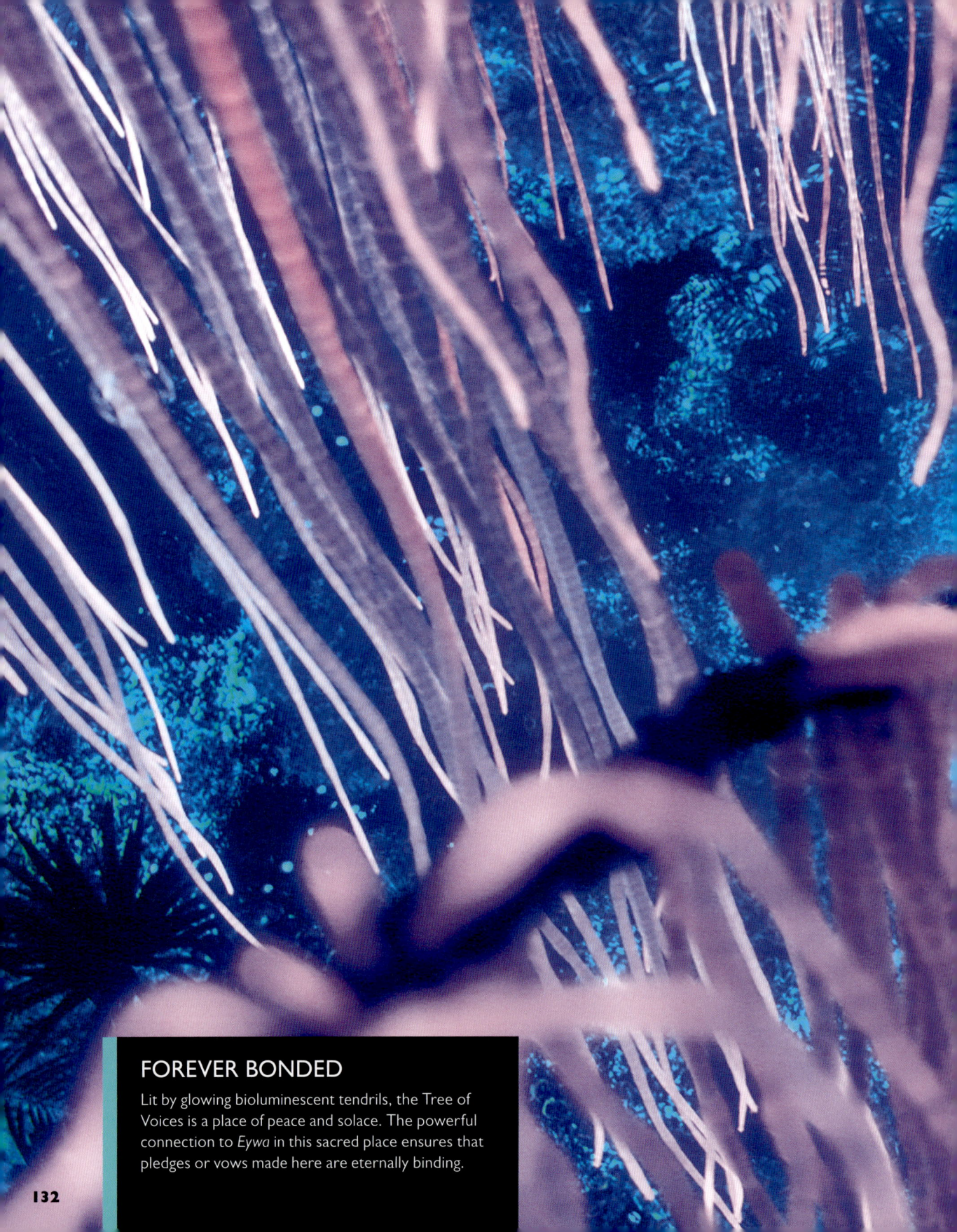

FOREVER BONDED

Lit by glowing bioluminescent tendrils, the Tree of Voices is a place of peace and solace. The powerful connection to *Eywa* in this sacred place ensures that pledges or vows made here are eternally binding.

Pilgrimage site
The Metkayina's Spirit Tree is located in the Cove of the Ancestors. In this sacred region, strong magnetic fields and high concentrations of unobtanium create fluxcons that hold floating islands above and below the water.

THE SPIRIT TREE

The sacred place for the Metkayina, where they commune with their ancestors and connect with *Eywa*

Known in the Na'vi language as *Ranteng Utralti*, the Metkayina's Spirit Tree is a towering yet delicate underwater structure that has a similar significance to the Reef People as the Tree of Voices (*Utraya Mokri*) or the Tree of Souls (*Vitraya Ramunong*) have to the Omatikaya clan of the rainforest. Other Na'vi clans have their own Spirit Trees, such as the Hulanta's Tree of Echoes in the Wetlands and the Rey'tanu's colorful Spirit Tree in the Highlands.

The Reef Na'vi attach to the Spirit Tree by intertwining their *kuru* to one of its fronds. The connected Na'vi receives oxygen through the neural bond, permitting long underwater sessions. Once connected, the Na'vi can access *Eywa*'s neural network, within which they "upload" and view their own memories and interact with the stored spirits of their ancestors. During this physically dissociated state of mind, Na'vi are paired with a diving partner to watch over and monitor them. The experience can be so emotionally impactful that afterward the Na'vi may require support from their diving partner to return to the surface.

Flora or fauna?
The Spirit Tree is an animal-like plant, or zooplantae. It has a nervous system that allows sentience and muscles that facilitate movement.

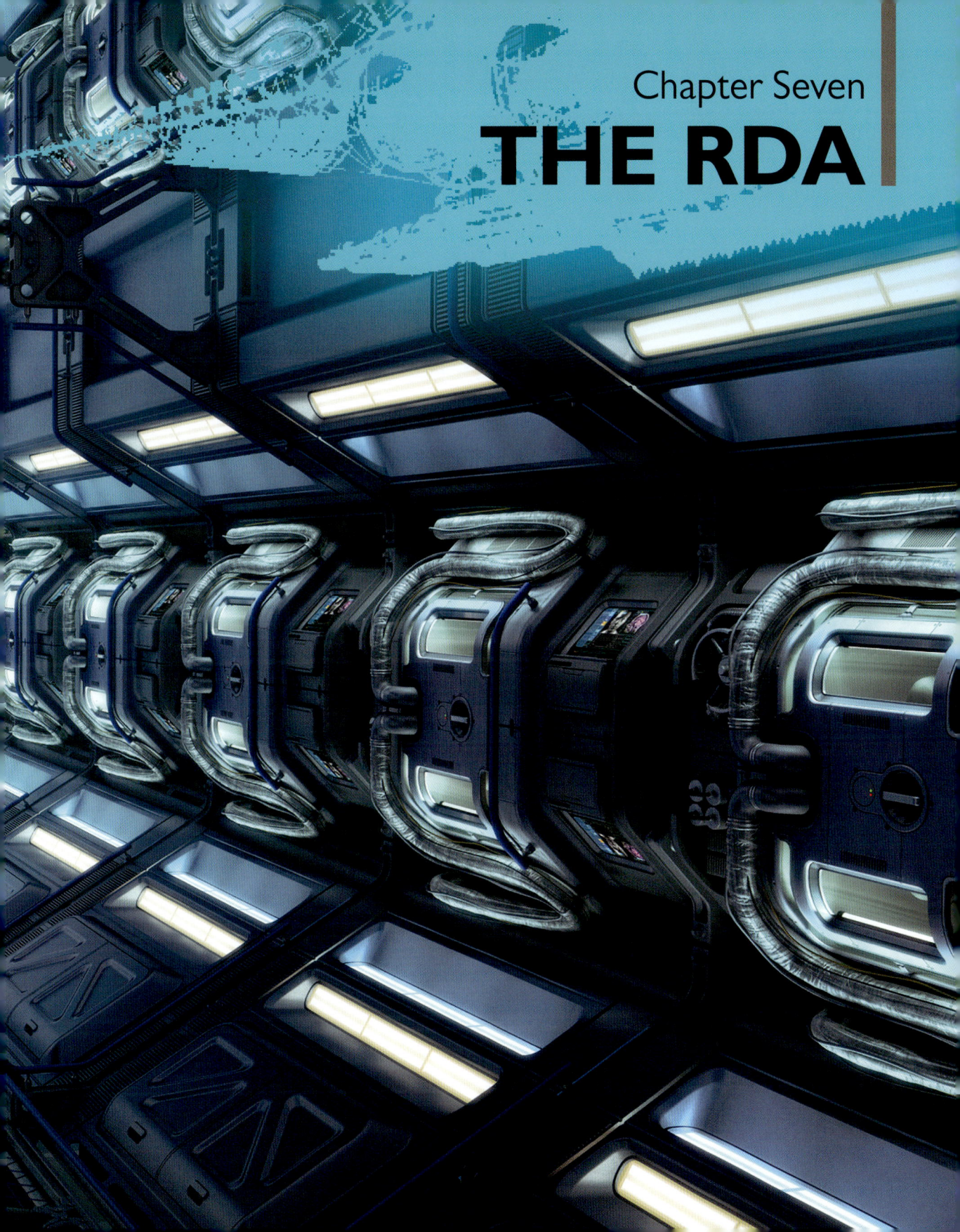

Chapter Seven
THE RDA

Data file

HULL NUMBER: 601-09
LENGTH: 4,929 ft (1,502.4 m)
WIDTH: 992 ft (302.3 m)
HEIGHT: 715 ft (218 m)
RANGE: 4.4 light years
POWER SOURCE: Hybrid fusion/matter-antimatter
CRUISING SPEED: 130,488 miles per sec (210,000 km per sec)

ISV VENTURE STAR

An engineering marvel that can traverse galaxies

The Interstellar Vehicle (ISV) *Venture Star*, along with the other ships of its class, represents the highest technological achievement in human history. The *Venture Star* is one of a multi-vehicle fleet that provides commercial space transportation between Earth and the Alpha Centauri star system. Like other ships of the Capital Star class, it is designed to carry a large payload of cargo and passengers to Alpha Centauri, and especially to the rich world of Pandora.

The ship's mission is to be part of a supply chain that enables the exploitation of Pandora's natural resources. The huge cost of these vessels is justified by human civilization's increasing reliance on unobtanium for key transportation technologies such as maglev and orbital mass launchers. Without the valuable commodity, interstellar commerce on this scale would not be possible. Unobtanium is used in the superconducting magnet arrays that contain and direct the ship's matter-antimatter-annihilation power source.

IDPS shielding

Unobtanium payload

Modular design
These Habitation—or "Hab"—modules contain the human passengers who are making the journey from Earth to Pandora.

Deep freeze
Dozens of passengers doze peacefully in artificially induced comas. Their bodies are kept safe in chilled cryovaults and are monitored by medics.

A STRUCTURAL MARVEL

The ship is propelled by two side-by-side engines. These are attached to a delicate truss leading to the payload section, which includes habitation for a crew of 25 people, up to 200 passengers in cryosleep, and a cargo hold. This is protected by the Interstellar Debris Protection System (IDPS), which comprises four angular flat plates stacked with space between them, all tethered to a central trunk. At full extension, the ship measures nearly a mile (1.5 km) long.

For reasons of scale and structure, the ship was constructed in Earth's atmosphere and designed to always remain in orbit—either Earth's or Pandora's. The ship is now too large and too fragile to land on the surface of any large celestial body with gravity. Instead, shuttle craft are used for sorties to planets.

Massive radiator structures dissipate engine heat into space

Coming and going
Owing to extremely long flight times, up to seven ISV vehicles are traveling to and from Pandora at any given time.

139

RETURN TO PANDORA

A new threat emerges 15 years after the RDA's defeat at the Battle of the Hallelujah Mountains

Bright lights in the sky signal the arrival of the ISV (Interstellar Vehicle) *Manifest Destiny*, along with 11 other inbound ships. Humans have returned to Pandora to establish a new home for their species in the wake of a despoiled and dying Earth.

Hovering in the sky, the RDA ships use enormous winches with miles of cables to lower Landing Modules to the lunar surface. As much as 40 stories tall, Landing Modules are cargo vehicles packed with a variety of construction robots, building materials, military assets, and thousands of human personnel. They facilitate the rapid construction of a new main operating base, known as Bridgehead City, which soon eclipses the size of Hell's Gate. Bridgehead is a beachhead for the intended human colonization of Pandora.

Efficient delivery
Lowered as "sling loads" by starships, Landing Modules can deliver massive payloads to Pandora at a quicker and more efficient rate than would be possible using Trans Atmospheric Vehicles (TAVs).

Deadly cargo
An Interstellar Vehicle uses its antimatter engines to hover in the sky while lowering a Landing Module to the surface.

Data file

MANUFACTURER: DF
MODEL: Landing Module
AFFILIATION: RDA CON-DEV
HEIGHT: 577 ft (176 m)
CREW: Up to 300
WEAPONS: Two XW460 Typhon Turrets; 40 mm autocannons; AG-MFM 335 missiles

Tough exterior
Thermal shielding protects the craft in space and during atmospheric descent.

Pylon supports
Shock-absorbing legs with adaptable feet deliver Landing Modules safely to the ground.

Troop egress
Heavily armed Sec-Ops forces are deployed via a hydraulic hatch.

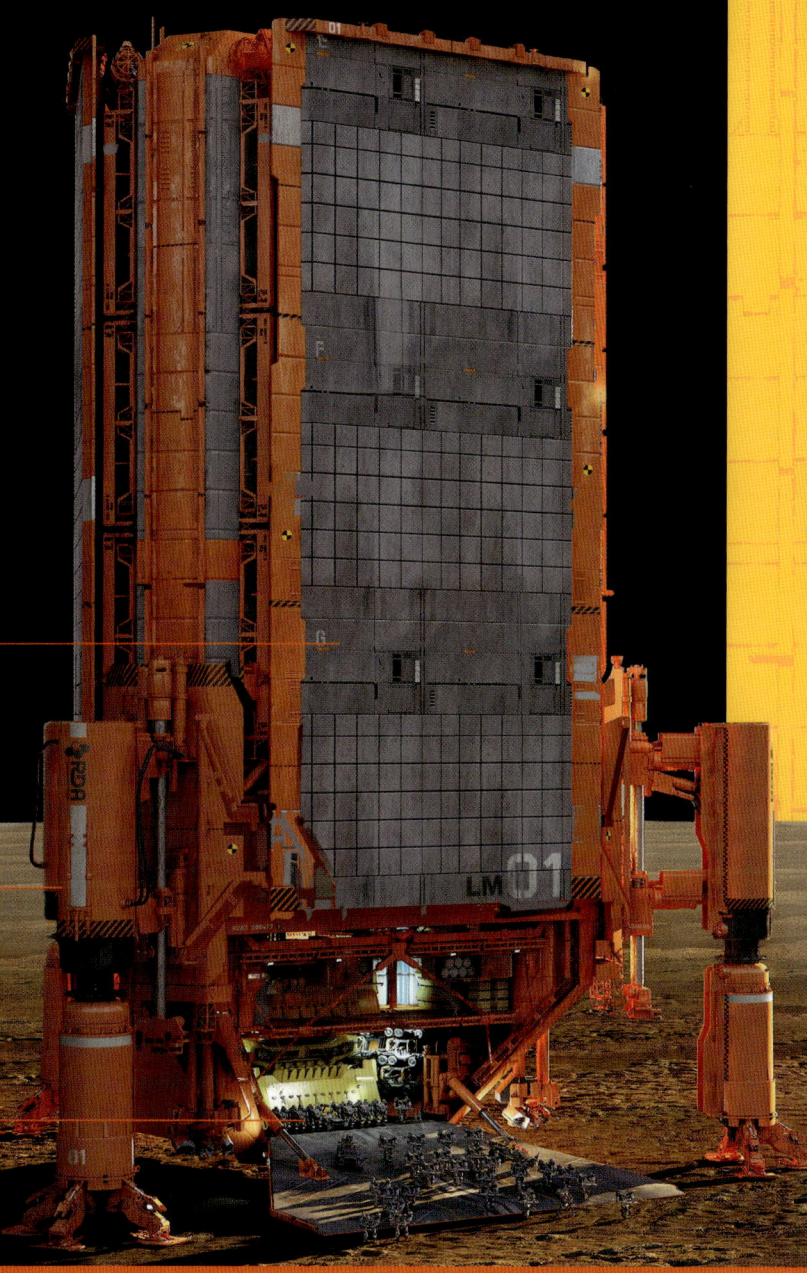

HEAVY PAYLOAD

Anticipating immediate hostile resistance, the RDA uses Landing Modules to shorten the timeframe for the establishment of new, heavily fortified bases of operation on Pandora. Each ruggedly built craft is packed with a customized load, including bulldozers and roadheaders for clearing and leveling landing sites, military assets for protecting building work, and modular architectural systems and defense walls. Human personnel are housed in cryosleep units and monitored on the long journey by small teams of med techs.

VALKYRIE SHUTTLE

Transporting cargo, supplies, and personnel between orbiting ISV starships and the surface of Pandora

The Valkyrie shuttle that takes new arrivals on the final leg of their journey to Pandora is classed as a TAV (Trans Atmospheric Vehicle), a general term for shuttles that carry cargo and passengers between orbit and the surface of a planet. The Valkyrie is roughly four times the size of an equivalent 21st-century Earth transport shuttle; however its mass is relatively small for its size due to the extremely strong, non-metallic composite material used in its fuselage. This material has high tensile strength, but weighs only one quarter of the permalloys used in previous shuttles. The ship's superstructure also uses carbon nanotube composite in key locations to maximize stability and help conserve fuel.

The Valkyrie's powerful, dual-mode fusion engine leaves a plume of energy so bright that at night its trajectory is visible from Hell's Gate almost all the way to orbit—it disappears over the horizon before orbital velocity is reached. The vessel reaches orbit in under ten minutes, but then takes an additional six hours to maneuver and dock with the ISV.

Data file

HULL NUMBER: SSTO-TAV-37
LENGTH: 334 ft (101.7 m)
WIDTH: 263 ft (80 m)
RANGE: 1,243 miles (2,000 km) in atmosphere
POWER SOURCE: Dual-mode fusion engine
CRUISING SPEED: More than 4,027 mph (64,820 kph) when leaving Pandora's gravitational field.

Deployment
The Valkyrie can lower a massive rear ramp for the unloading of large vehicles and AMP Suits.

Hauling cargo
Practicality is prioritized over passenger comfort in the Valkyrie's cargo bay. Fold-down seats allow for maximum storage room.

AN RDA WORKHORSE

The Valkyrie's cargo bay is packed with netting to secure payloads to the walls. It also contains rollers built into the floor to facilitate unloading and seats for traveling personnel. On incoming flights, the Valkyrie may deliver troops, AMP Suits (see pp. 162–63), supplies, and specialized electronic and lab equipment that cannot be manufactured on Pandora. But its most important mission is transporting refined unobtanium from the surface of Pandora to an orbiting ISV. Without this capability, there would be little or no human presence on Pandora. It is also the only possible ride back to the mothership, and thus provides an integral link for humans starting the long journey back to Earth.

Air support
Slightly more than a third of the site is taken up by the shuttle runway, vertical takeoff and landing (VTOL) pads, and associated support facilities.

Mining operations
The strip mine adjacent to Hell's Gate is the largest source of unobtanium in current use. The area looks like a large, ugly gash torn in the forested valley.

HELL'S GATE

A concrete and steel blight on the pristine landscape of Pandora

Officially named the Resources Development Administration Extra-Solar Colony, the place humans on Pandora call home is universally referred to as Hell's Gate. Its purpose: unobtanium mining and scientific research of the planet's biosphere. Hell's Gate is also the nerve center of the RDA's Avatar Program.

Run with military precision, Hell's Gate has a population of 2,500 and comprises barracks for Sec-Ops staff, administrative offices, a commissary, training facilities, an airtight condominium for senior staff, and facilities for weapons and vehicles. An unpressurized section between the research labs and the landing zone has specific areas designated for use by members of the Avatar Program, including the Long House where they sleep; areas for athletics training; areas for field sports; and areas for planting, gardening, and agriculture.

DEFENSIVE MEASURES

Hell's Gate is in a constant state of siege because of the toxic Pandoran environment and its dangerous wildlife. A pentagonal perimeter fence surrounds the complex. Weapons towers protect against intrusions from the air, land, or underground. A cleared strip 98 ft (30 m) wide surrounds the base, patrolled by plant-clearing machinery that keeps the jungle at bay through regular administration of acidic mining byproducts.

Abandoned base
After the RDA's retreat in 2154, the jungle reclaims Hell's Gate and the Na'vi traverse it with impunity.

145

AN ENCROACHING MENACE

As a Valkyrie shuttle comes in to land, the full expanse of the human colony known as Hell's Gate is visible. The gray concrete and steel industrial compound is a stark contrast to the lush green Pandoran surroundings. The RDA has set up perimeter alarms and other defenses to stop rainforest creatures and plants from encroaching upon the areas it has made habitable for humans.

BRIDGEHEAD

Ground zero of the RDA's second attempt at the colonization of Pandora

Vastly larger than the RDA's first colonial outpost on Pandora, Hell's Gate (see pp. 144–45), the organization's new flagship installation, Bridgehead, is an impregnable, city-sized base of operations. A beachhead for full-blown human colonization, this extraterrestrial "boom town" is a hive of chaotic construction—and will remain so for several years, while the raw materials needed for concrete and steel are extracted on the planet. Bridgehead's innumerable subcontractors—all keen to make a profit—are overseen by an administrative entity called CON-DEV (Consolidated Development), which is also in charge of construction hexbots, robotic cranes, and heavy-lift airships. Bridgehead embodies the RDA's motto of "Building Tomorrow" and some call it the last hope for a dying Earth.

Data file

BRIDGEHEAD DIAMETER: 6 miles (9.6 km)

ACCESS: 3 land gates; 2 sea gates; 1 river gate

TARGET POPULATION: 2 million (upon completion)

OPS CENTER CIVILIAN PERSONNEL: Approx. 180

OPS CENTER SEC-OPS PERSONNEL: Approx. 120

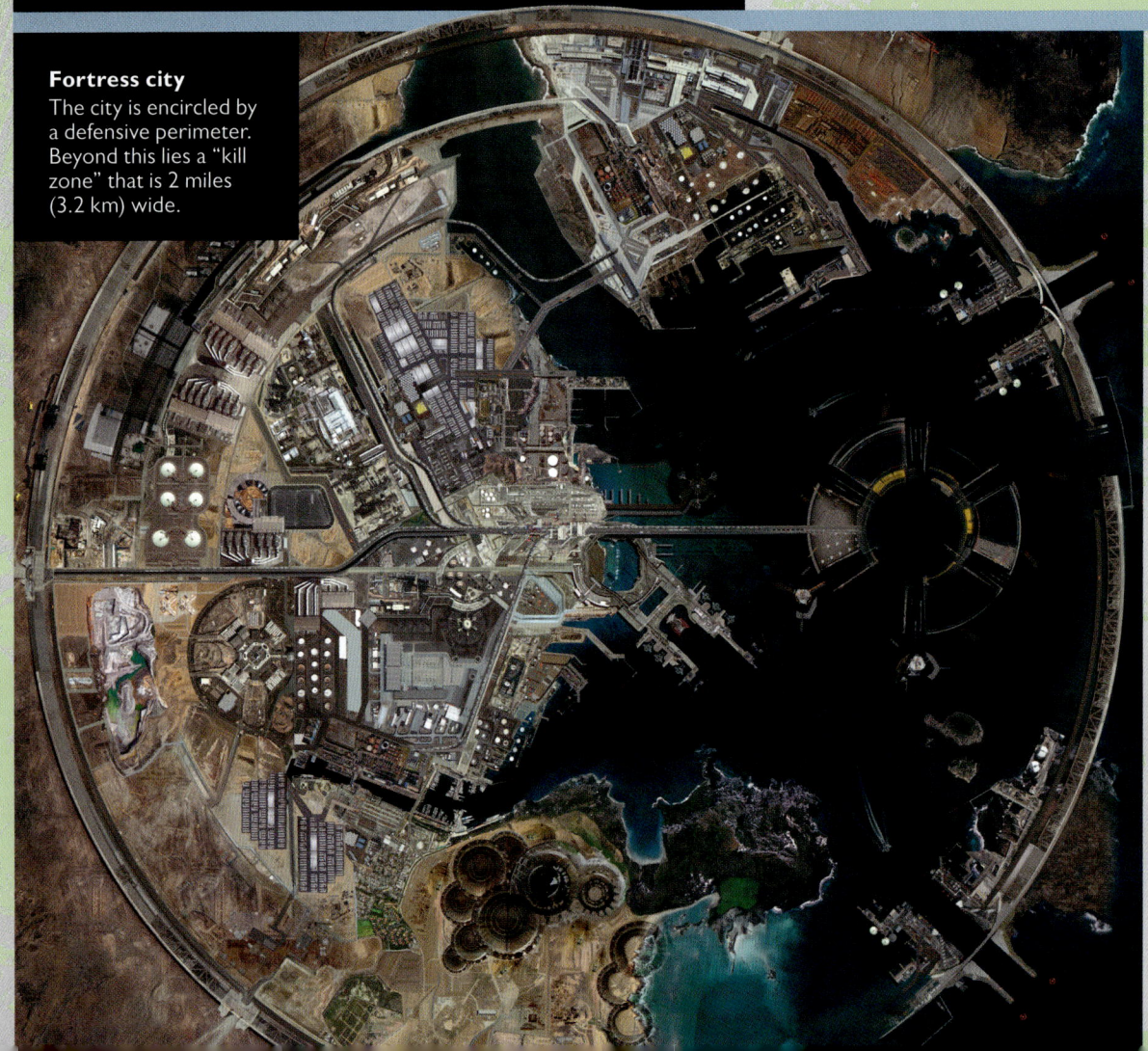

Fortress city
The city is encircled by a defensive perimeter. Beyond this lies a "kill zone" that is 2 miles (3.2 km) wide.

OPS CENTER AND SCI-OPS COMPLEX

In Bridgehead's expansive, high-tech Ops Center, civilian and military personnel work hand in hand to coordinate the RDA's efforts on Pandora. The planning and control of all aspects of business, from mining and superspeed construction to Sec-Ops (Security Operations) defense and escort functions, is conducted within an airport terminal-sized communications center bristling with complex data displays. On the Holofloor, personnel can step right into the data in all its complexity and manipulate it in real time to facilitate rapid and effective command decision-making. Within the Sci-Ops (Science Operations) campus, the NeuroLab showcases the most advanced neural scanning and stimulus system that RDA scientists have ever operated.

Holofloor
The command zone of the Ops Center is the Holofloor, where senior command staff review data from all over the RDA's operation—video feeds, maps, GPS vehicle traffic, and archived or live 3D scans of environments.

Neurolab
In the Sci-Ops campus, a high-tech medical suite contains a NeuroSect E7.2T scanner, in which brain data can be collated and fed to a real-time walk-in holo display.

Heavy lifters
Construction blimps move large loads. Their lift systems allow almost indefinite hovering while massive payloads are lowered.

Swarm assemblers
RDA CON-DEV's latest-generation robotic swarm assemblers make possible every type of on-site fabrication with a minimum of human labor and management. Each model of assembler carries its own host of cameras and sensors, but the machines work together as a coordinated group.

CONSTRUCTION

A variety of robotic machines allow on-site fabrication with a minimum of human labor and management

Managed by the RDA's CON-DEV (Consolidated Development) wing, the construction of Bridgehead and its supporting outposts is heavily automated and algorithmic, doing away with all human-operated RDA remote vehicles. Hundreds of robotic heavy lift blimps, cranes, and swarm assemblers stack prefabricated structures into enormous power and processing plants, while a web of high-speed maglev train lines delivers materials and robots across the vast site. From robotic raw material extraction and high-tech manufacturing to swarm assembly of enormous structures, the new style of RDA construction is productive and highly organized. This is crucial for human expansion, since sending people to Pandora is a slow and expensive process, while construction robots can be manufactured in almost unlimited numbers on-world.

Hexbot Heavy
The workhorse of the assembler fleet, the Hexbot Heavy is a multi-role swarm assembler around the size of a large dog.

Frontier town
Bridgehead is growing rapidly, aided by in-situ 3D printing of concrete architecture and components and the use of lightweight, modular, inflatable temporary buildings.

Big Quad
The Big Quad large assembler uses its two powerful arms and grippers to carry the heaviest building components.

Hauler
The Hauler support bot delivers pipes, fittings, struts, panels, and utility components—and a myriad of fasteners to put them together.

MC-RA 220
This robotic crane is over 300 ft (90 m) tall and uses its telescoping crane boom to reach over large-area sites.

Hexbot Light
This Hexbot Light focuses on welding, grinding, riveting, and even painting. What this mini swarm assembler lacks in size it makes up for in efficiency.

151

ROBOTIC SWARM

Hexbots operate in intelligent, coordinated swarms, guided by a suite of sophisticated and layered algorithms. This way of working can reduce the time it takes to construct an entire building to mere days.

Colonel Miles Quaritch

A Force Reconnaissance Marine turned corporate security operator, Colonel Quaritch runs the RDA's Sec-Ops on Pandora. Quaritch has been hardened by a relentlessly tough military life. He is a veteran soldier who has fought without ever really having a cause worth fighting for. Now, Quaritch thinks he has found one: The survival of the human race, which he feels far outweighs the needs of native Pandoran species. No doubt influenced by his new RDA employers' unbridled greed, Quaritch is almost without empathy, meaning he has no qualms about destroying anything he can't—or won't—understand.

Attacked by a viperwolf on his first day on Pandora, Quaritch forms an abiding hatred for Pandora's wildlife, as well as its indigenous inhabitants. He wears the scars he received that day as a badge of pride. They remind him of the dangers that lurk on this "paradise" moon and of his own fortitude.

Quaritch is impatient to relocate the Na'vi from Hometree so that the unobtanium beneath it can be mined. This stems as much from his desire to accomplish his job and protect his troops as enmity toward the Na'vi. Killed in action by Neytiri, Quaritch's consciousness is downloaded into a clone Recombinant body (see pp 186–87).

Parker Selfridge

The head administrator of the RDA's operation on Pandora, Parker Selfridge embodies the stereotype of a blinkered corporate executive. He is an adequate manager from the standpoint of generating paperwork and overseeing the day-to-day operations of the Hell's Gate colony, however he is incapable of seeing the bigger picture.

Selfridge is not a particularly evil man; he is simply a product of corporate hubris and entitlement. He prefers practicing his putting to listening to Dr. Grace Augustine's considered arguments. Her pleas to treat Pandora and its wonders with respect thus fall on deaf ears. As far as Selfridge is concerned, the RDA's mandate is simple: Obtain the unobtanium. However, when the Na'vi win the first Pandoran War, Parker is sent back to Earth as punishment, where he bides his time until his return to Pandora.

Administrator, not adventurer
Selfridge stays within the confines of the RDA colony, viewing Pandora's landscape only via holograms.

RDA AND SEC-OPS PERSONNEL

Keeping Hell's Gate safe from any and all Pandoran lifeforms

Hell's Gate is home to hundreds upon hundreds of civilians, mining contractors, researchers, and other support staff in the employ of the RDA. In overall control of the base is the RDA's administrative chief Parker Selfridge. The RDA's Sec-Ops (Security Operations) division is responsible for keeping all personnel safe from Pandora's potentially deadly flora and fauna. Fronted by the grizzled, scarred visage of Colonel Miles Quaritch, the Sec-Ops team constantly patrols the terrain and airspace around Hell's Gate. The RDA's private military force is armed to the teeth with specialized equipment, like the Scorpion Gunship and VTOL Samson.

Sec-Ops is not only the first and last line of defense against any Pandoran insurgencies; it provides security details for the Sci-Ops division when its researchers are out in the field, as well as protection for unobtanium mining operations.

Corporal Lyle Wainfleet

Wainfleet embodies the concept of "might makes right," believing an AMP Suit grants him supreme moral authority. Killed when a hammerhead titanothere rams into his AMP Suit, Wainfleet is reborn as a Recom warrior (see pp. 186–87).

On borrowed time
Wainfleet is the epitome of the occupying military as ugly aggressor.

Trudy Chacón

Trudy is a cargo transport pilot. Although not forthcoming with details of her past, her experience suggests she has previously worked for a military or paramilitary organization. However, Trudy does not have much in common with Colonel Quaritch or her security force co-workers, having a greater rapport with the scientists in the Avatar Program. Her relationship with scientist Dr. Norm Spellman even becomes romantic.

Like the rest of the Sci-Ops team, Trudy is forced to choose sides in the growing conflict between the RDA and the Na'vi. She comes down decisively on the Na'vi side during the Battle of the Hallelujah Mountains. While Norm, the man she loves, is running for his life through the jungle in his avatar form, Trudy sacrifices her life by steering her SA-2 Samson transport helicopter straight into the belly of Quaritch's lead attack ship. Her courageous intervention forces Quaritch to delay his attack long enough to save the Tree of Souls from destruction.

Honor bound
Wisecracking, sassy, and fiercely loyal, Trudy Chacón is very much her own woman—and nobody's fool.

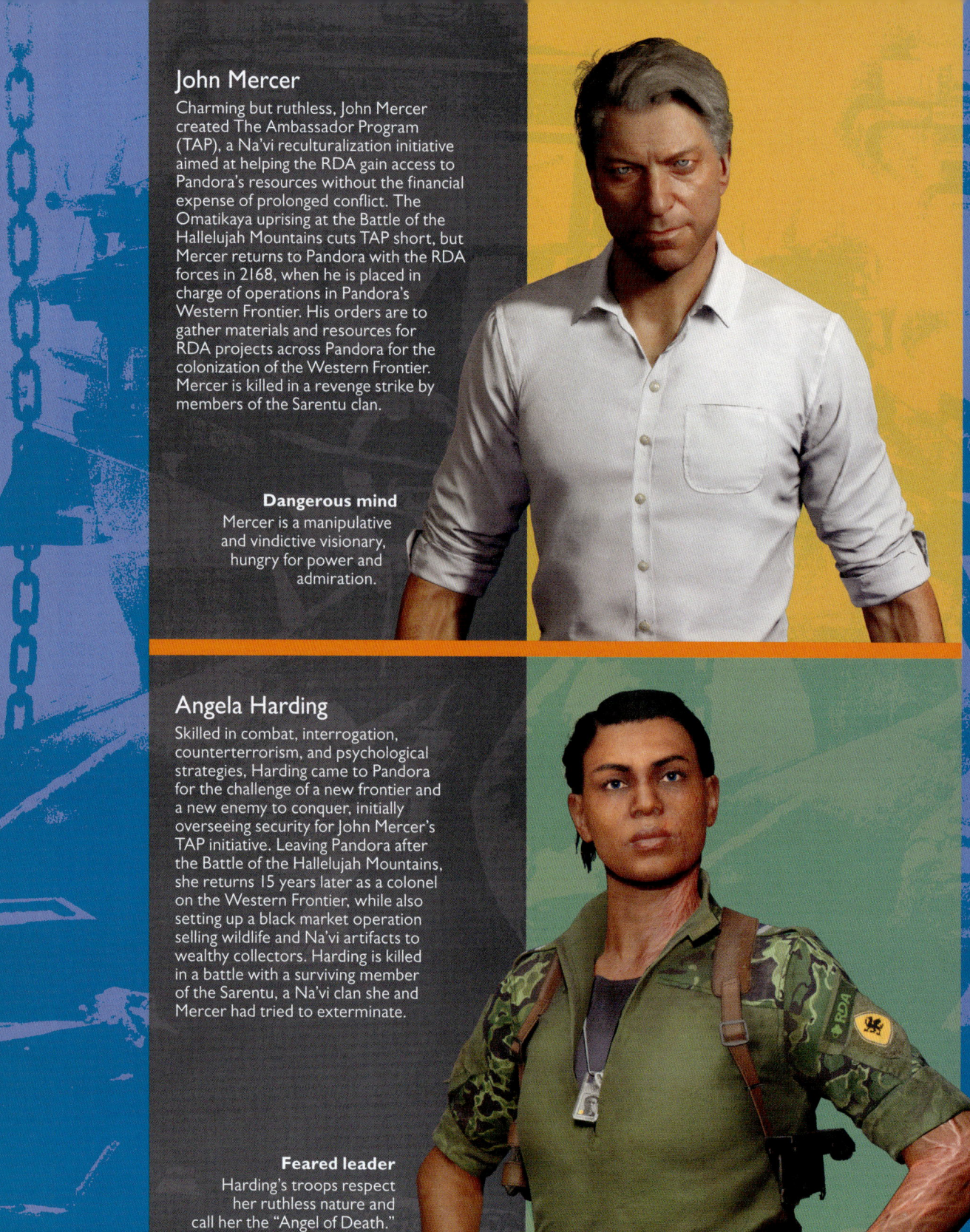

John Mercer

Charming but ruthless, John Mercer created The Ambassador Program (TAP), a Na'vi reculturalization initiative aimed at helping the RDA gain access to Pandora's resources without the financial expense of prolonged conflict. The Omatikaya uprising at the Battle of the Hallelujah Mountains cuts TAP short, but Mercer returns to Pandora with the RDA forces in 2168, when he is placed in charge of operations in Pandora's Western Frontier. His orders are to gather materials and resources for RDA projects across Pandora for the colonization of the Western Frontier. Mercer is killed in a revenge strike by members of the Sarentu clan.

Dangerous mind
Mercer is a manipulative and vindictive visionary, hungry for power and admiration.

Angela Harding

Skilled in combat, interrogation, counterterrorism, and psychological strategies, Harding came to Pandora for the challenge of a new frontier and a new enemy to conquer, initially overseeing security for John Mercer's TAP initiative. Leaving Pandora after the Battle of the Hallelujah Mountains, she returns 15 years later as a colonel on the Western Frontier, while also setting up a black market operation selling wildlife and Na'vi artifacts to wealthy collectors. Harding is killed in a battle with a surviving member of the Sarentu, a Na'vi clan she and Mercer had tried to exterminate.

Feared leader
Harding's troops respect her ruthless nature and call her the "Angel of Death."

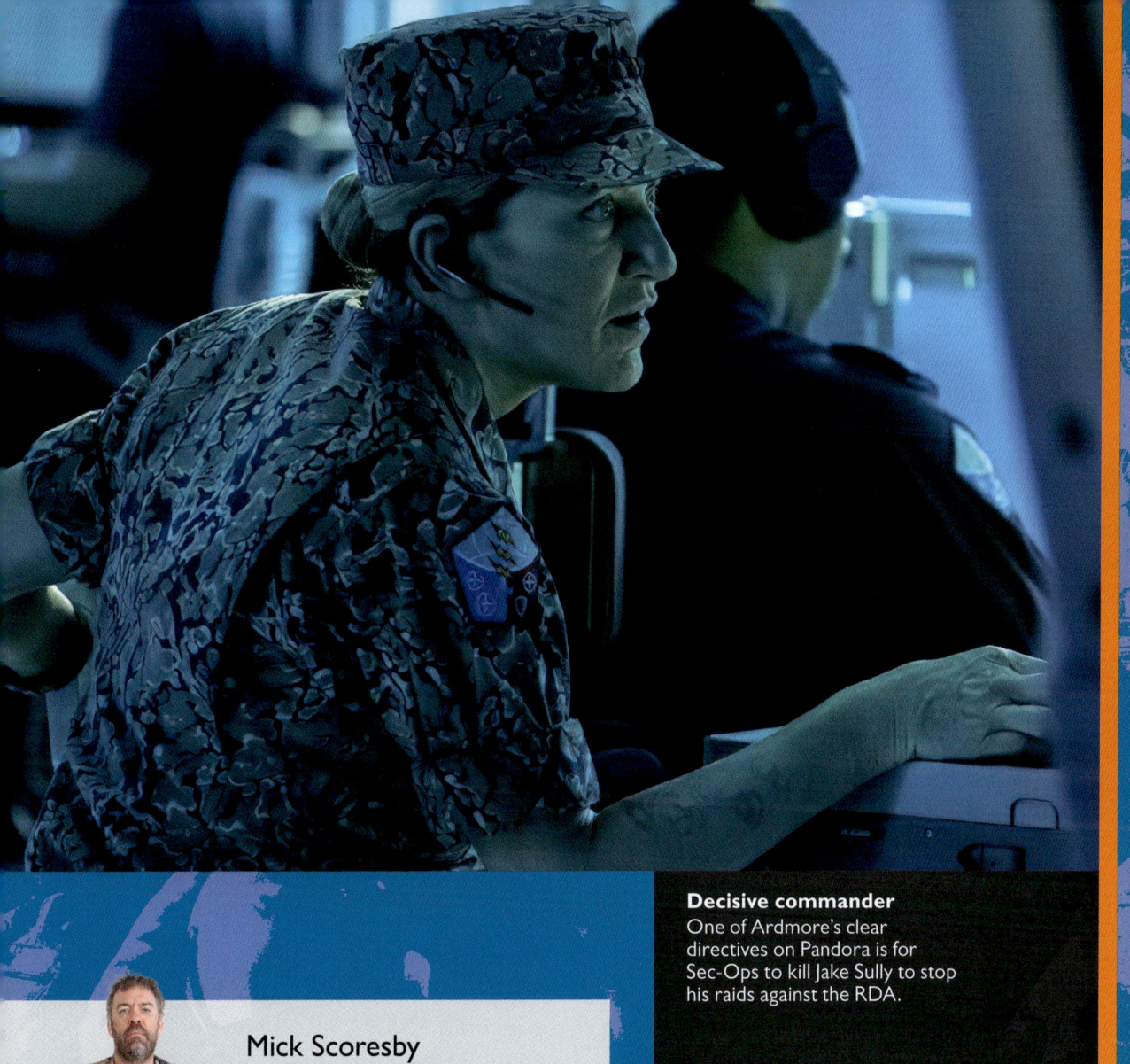

Decisive commander
One of Ardmore's clear directives on Pandora is for Sec-Ops to kill Jake Sully to stop his raids against the RDA.

Mick Scoresby
An aquatic big-game hunter, Mick Scoresby is hired by the RDA to hunt and harvest *tulkun* for their human lifespan-enhancing *amrita*. His mission on Pandora places him in charge of a fleet of sea vessels, including large SeaDragon ships. Recom warrior Miles Quaritch, however, quickly conscripts Scoresby to hunt down the Sullys.

Ocean hunter
Scoresby is thrilled to be hunting large ocean creatures again because the practice has long expired back on Earth.

Frances Ardmore
The RDA's new Expeditionary Force Commander, Frances Ardmore, is charged with the RDA/Sec-Ops' new top priority: retaking Pandora to make it humanity's new home. She is a well-educated and practiced political strategist, with a manner that conveys intelligence and mental agility. She is not only highly capable in combat but also a masterful thinker and planner. Unlike her predecessor, Colonel Miles Quaritch, who is obsessive and monomaniacal, Ardmore is detached and unemotional. In these desperate times, Ardmore is prepared to do whatever it takes.

DEVASTATION

A lone survivor stands amid the charred remains of the once glorious and majestic Hometree after the RDA's brutal military assault.

RDA MILITARY VEHICLES

The RDA's Sec-Ops division bristles with state-of-the-art war machines

The Sec-Ops division of the RDA is the first and last line of defense against the hostile flora, fauna, and inhabitants of Pandora. As Colonel Quaritch notes in his "welcome speech" to new recruits: "Out beyond that fence every living thing that crawls, flies, or squats in the mud wants to kill you and eat your eyes for jujubes." With that in mind, the RDA has outfitted its Security Operations division with the latest-available military technology to protect its assets.

Vehicles are manufactured on-site at Hell's Gate in a massive 3D-printer facility known as the Grinder. If a Scorpion Gunship is taken down by some Na'vi warriors riding banshees, the Grinder simply uses local natural resources to extrude the necessary parts to assemble a new one to replenish the fleet.

SA-2 Samson
Designed for mostly non-combat missions, the Samson features minimal armament and is used to drop supplies and personnel at distant field sites, including delivering avatars for interaction with the Na'vi.

Wyvern Troop Transport
The RDA uses this eight-rotor heavy transport aircraft to deploy troops and AMPs into hostile territory and for general close air support.

AT-99 Scorpion Gunship
Round-the-clock Scorpion patrols are crucial to the defense of RDA assets. The vehicle's retro design functions well in Pandora's harsh environment.

C-21 Dragon Assault Ship
An aerial weapons platform capable of inflicting heavy casualties, the Dragon has been upgraded for use in Pandora's powerful electromagnetic fields.

ALL BASES COVERED

Pandora is a world of diverse habitats—everything from dense rainforests to snowy tundra, from grasslands to vast oceans. The RDA is determined that its arsenal of equipment should be as capable of fully functioning at any location on Pandora as it would be on Earth. All the organization's military vehicles are capable of formidable firepower, ensuring that local resistance, whether by the Na'vi or in the form of animal attacks, is ruthlessly crushed.

67-1A Liquid Environment Transport
The 67-1A is a four-person craft that provides armed escort for larger transports. The RDA uses them to carry small teams of field operators, avatars, or scientists across water.

JL-723 Swan
The Ground Assault Vehicle (GAV) JL-723, or Swan, is the RDA's all-terrain vehicle for land combat. Bristling with weaponry, it can travel at high speeds and is armored with permalloy.

Data file

OFFICIAL NAME: MK-6 Armored Mobile Platform Suit

FUNCTION: Ambulatory weapons platform for military and civilian operations in hostile and toxic environments.

HEIGHT: 13 ft 8 in (4.2 m)

WEIGHT: 3,748 lbs (1,700 kg)

WEAPONS: Detachable GAU-90 30 mm cannon (ammo belt runs through flexible feed chute); optional flamethrower, large ceramic knife

Size matters
The relative heights of an average human being, a Na'vi hunter, and the AMP Suit emphasize the latter's intimidating presence.

Raw power
Safe in the suit, the driver can punch through a tree trunk, lift a massive cargo crate, or launch a military attack.

AMP SUIT

A walking, hydraulic, armored, near-invulnerable exo-suit

The Amplified Mobility Platform (or "AMP" Suit) is a distant descendant of military exoskeletons first used on Earth in the mid-21st century. It was improved during military service in combat theaters over the decades, and its capabilities have proved invaluable in Pandora's toxic atmosphere and dangerous environment. The AMP Suit is a multipurpose machine, able to duplicate all the functions of an infantry soldier. Since soldiers perform many tasks besides operating weapons, the AMP Suit needs the same functionality as a human: two legs, two arms, and highly dexterous hands. This design enables a wide range of functions and also allows the suit to operate a variety of weapons. The driver controls the suit via high-tech armatures: for example, when the driver moves his arm, the suit instantly responds.

UTILITY SUIT—A NEW BEGINNING

Generations after the conflict between the Na'vi and the humans of the RDA, the eco-tourism company Alpha Centauri Expeditions (ACE) begins sending travelers to Pandora. To help with exploration, protection of the Pandoran ecosystem, and education, ACE commissions the Utility Suit, or "Ute Suit." This is a highly modified and more sophisticated version of the old RDA exoskeleton. Unlike the RDA's AMP Suit, the Ute Suit is only used for peaceful research and study.

War no more
Visitors to the lush Mo'ara Valley will see ACE employees in Ute Suits working to conserve the Pandoran landscape.

AMP SUIT VARIANTS

A series of powerful, new-gen AMP Suits used by the RDA to seek and destroy enemies

The RDA has developed a number of variant AMP Suits to use in missions such as the campaign to colonize the Western Frontier. Executive Vice President of Frontier Operations John Mercer has led the design of these upgraded AMP models, some of which are equipped with high-impact cockpit canopies and enhanced weaponry, including napalm grenade launchers and flamethrowers. Although the external chemical fuel tanks that power this volatile weaponry are vulnerable to attack—potentially causing collateral damage to RDA pilots—Mercer and the RDA consider the risk worth taking: these fearsome AMP Suits offer a squad an enhanced ability to cut a swathe through difficult landscape, put down local opposition, and defeat strong enemy positions.

AMP Commando
One of the most powerful AMP Suits used by the RDA, the Commando utilizes enhanced cockpit armor and advanced sensors to seek and destroy enemies.

AMP Grenadier
This AMP Suit is equipped with multiple grenade launchers to attack enemies from short or long ranges, increasing the strength of a squad.

AMP Assault
The standard AMP model is not as light or cost-effective as the Combat Exo, but is preferred by management and pilots as it comes with better armor and a protective cockpit canopy without sacrificing agility.

Mercer's Guard AMP
A unique AMP type created to John Mercer's specifications, this flameproof, highly mobile suit lays waste to the battlefield with napalm grenades and a flamer pistol.

Combat Exo
Unpopular with most pilots, the lightest and most cost-efficient AMP model has a risky open cockpit, designed to reduce the machine's overall weight.

AMP Pyro
This close-quarters combat AMP is equipped with flamethrowers as its primary weapon. The cockpit canopy has been reinforced to protect the pilot against the heat.

SKEL

A stripped-down version of the AMP Suit used in the RDA colonization effort

The Skel, or Skel Suit, is a mechanical exoskeleton, or motorized stilt-walker, that makes a human as tall, strong, and fast as a Na'vi, and able to shoulder an arsenal of high-caliber assault weapons or even a devastating flamethrower. Every Skel trooper is armed for success against Na'vi and the thick-skinned wild beasts of Pandora with a Skel AR (assault rifle) and its shorter-barreled brother, the Skel Bullpup—weapons that have been specifically scaled up for the large frame of a Skel. Operators can also be equipped with a flamethrower for clearing vegetation—and for burning homes in order to force Indigenous peoples into RDA compliance.

COMBAT AND CIVILIAN USES

The Skel is a multipurpose capability amplifier for industrial and military applications. It can operate safely around unprotected human personnel due to its lightweight manufacture, excellent driver situational awareness, and automated collision-avoidance features. The moderate size of a Skel means it can use airlocks and corridors built for humans, unlike the lumbering AMP Suit. In the marine context, aboard a SeaDragon a Skel can dextrously wrangle cargo, chains, and other heavy equipment as part of vehicle maintenance or *tulkun*-hunting operations.

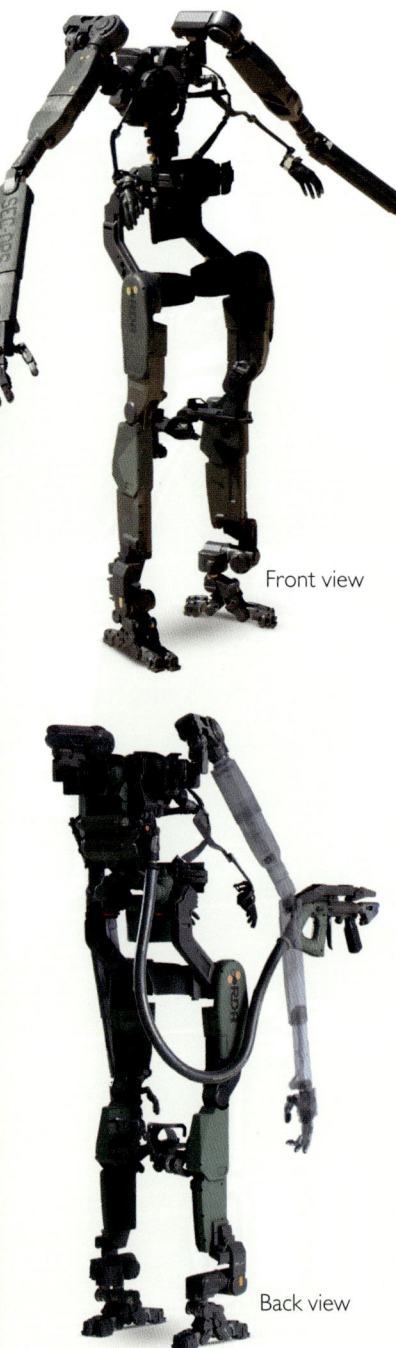

Front view

Back view

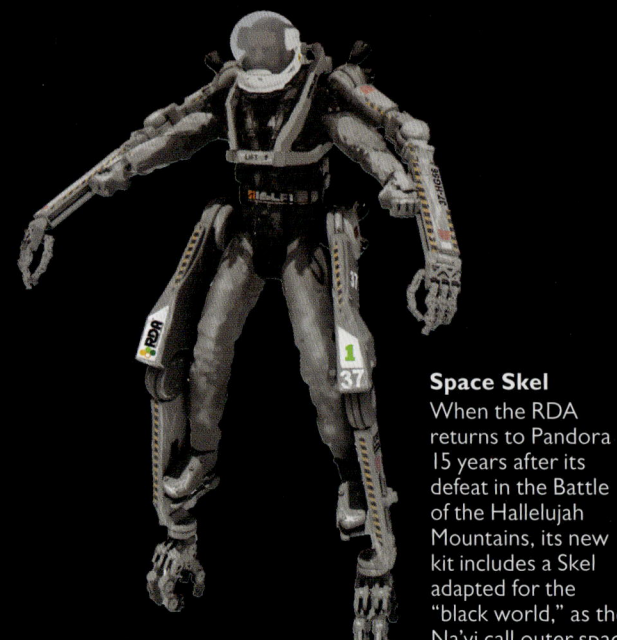

Space Skel
When the RDA returns to Pandora 15 years after its defeat in the Battle of the Hallelujah Mountains, its new kit includes a Skel adapted for the "black world," as the Na'vi call outer space.

Enhanced abilities
A Skel Suit's robotic skeleton can do heavy work with minimal operator exertion, while its hands can perform even the most precise technical work. The machine's semi-prehensile feet can grasp terrain and roots for aggressive forest running.

Data file

MANUFACTURER: UKII
MODEL: EXO-32 Light Mobility Platform
HEIGHT: 9 ft 6 in (2.9 m)
MAX. SPEED: 20 mph (32 kph)
WEAPONS: Skel AR; Skel Bullpup; flamethrower; Bullet Hose

Combat roles
Equipped with a Y70 Bullpup rifle, Skel engagements are mostly at firearm range. However, some operators also train in robotic martial arts techniques.

Automatic weapons

MBS-9M .50 cal Hydra
This Hydra's primary function is as a door gun on RDA gunships. It can also be used as a handheld light machine gun by ground forces.

MBS-22A automated sentry gun
Sited in watchtowers, these weapons ensure any attacks on Hell's Gate are met with devastating firepower.

GS-221 .30 cal light machine gun
This weapon features technology that allows the shooter to program a bullet to hit targets not entirely in line of sight.

Grenades

The RDA employs various grenades for different purposes, including incendiary, personnel, and smoke. The green plastic "spoon" flies off when released, activating the timer; this has a delay adjustment dial that can be set to between two and eight seconds before the grenade explodes.

Incendiary grenade

Personnel grenade

Smoke grenade

Handguns

SN-9 WASP revolver
This gun's extra punch is of particular use on Pandora, where many of the dangerous animals are large and cannot always be brought down with standard RDA sidearms.

RDA sidearm
This small-caliber (8 mm) weapon focuses on simplicity and reliability over fast firing rates and sheer power.

Explosive devices

Daisy cutter
A large-scale explosive device that links multiple incendiary devices together for maximum destructive effect—hence its nickname "daisy chain."

Hydra 70-rocket
These 70 mm rockets are armed with various high explosives, white phosphorous, and TDCMD (Tail-Drag Cluster Munitions Dispersement) for use against indigenous fauna.

AMP Suit weaponry

GAU-90 .30mm cannon
This can be used as a conventional weapon against larger creatures; however, its high explosives have proved very effective when clearing paths through dense foliage.

BushBoss FD-3
This flamethrower is primarily used to clear an area of trees and plants prior to the use of earth movers. It is also used to repel wildlife and to terrify Na'vi attackers.

AMP Suit knife
Attached to the underside of an AMP Suit's arm, this high-tensile alloy cutter is primarily used to clear paths through jungle.

Combat shotgun
This weapon utilizes a wide array of 20 mm munitions, such as air-burst grenades, high-explosive rounds, and armor-penetrating rounds.

RDA WEAPONRY

High-tech armaments designed to tackle the toughest missions the 22nd century has to offer

The RDA Sec-Ops division on Pandora boasts that it is ready for anything. It maintains a mighty arsenal to deal with native Omatikaya warriors determined to prevent the RDA despoiling their homeland. Sec-Ops also has to deal with potentially deadly attacks from the air, on land, and on the sea by Pandora's aggressive wildlife.

Massive machine guns command the perimeter of the RDA's Hell's Gate base. Sec-Ops personnel also have a range of weaponry at their disposal. As well as armored vehicles, they can employ bombs, missiles, grenades, flamethrowers, automatic weapons, and weaponized battle suits—more than sufficient to repel onslaughts by creatures such as flying stingbats and to crush Omatikaya resistance. Sec-Ops' ruthless chief, Colonel Miles Quaritch, is supremely confident that his men's bullets will prevail over Na'vi bows and arrows. Every time.

CARB weapons system

CARB sub-machine gun
Primarily used inside the Hell's Gate compound by Sec-Ops personnel; also issued to pilots and vehicle drivers.

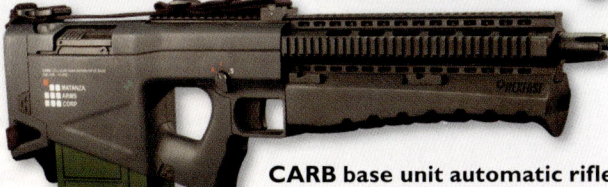

CARB base unit automatic rifle
This can be modified with an extended barrel, 20 mm munition launcher, and day/night stabilized optical zoom scope.

CARB automatic rifle with underslung shotgun
This is the above base unit with an added modular CARB shotgun attachment.

RDA tech

Sat comm
Contained within a rugged hard case, this sat comm includes a wireless handset for radio comms.

Field pad
This rugged device uses encrypted comms and a globally networked data interface.

Transponder
The IFF (Identify Friend or Foe) transponder allows RDA troopers and vehicles to identify themselves to automated defense systems.

Datapads
Advanced datapads use the same pseudoholographic display tech found in RDA computer workstations.

Bio scanner
The life-saving CR-4 diagnostic sys is equipped with a multipurpose scan wand.

Guns and rifles

Z-33 pistol
The Z-33 is the standard firearm used by RDA Sec-Ops Troops.

Skel M69-AR
This assault rifle is designed for the large build of a Recom or Skel Suit.

SN-9 WASP revolver
This revolver is not an RDA-issue firearm but is used by Colonel Miles Quaritch.

EV assault rifle
Used by Sec-Ops troops, this weapon features holographic sights and a grenade launcher.

Drone
Used for scouting, exploration, or surveillance, drones use dual rotorblades to fly and are armed with an assault gun and taser projector.

Hellhound
The RDA deploys packs of tracker bots, known as Hellhounds, to hunt down targets. Their red optical sensors include night vision and infrared, while their armor casing protects against Na'vi hunting bows. The bot's electrified metallic jaws take down targets with maximum force.

Other weaponry

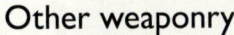

Guided munition
The AM6-75L "Fire Arrow" is a guided missile specialized for use against a wide variety of targets.

Recom AR mag
This detachable storage device feeds rounds into the chambers of Recom assault rifles.

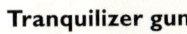

Missile launcher
The Toxon-81 anti-aircraft missile launcher has been adapted for Pandoran use with targeting to lock onto living beings.

Grenade
Issued to RDA troops, this handheld explosive device features a delayed fuse with a flip-open top section.

Tranquilizer gun
The Y6 is a model of stun gun designed specifically for use on Pandora.

Combat /utility knife
The K-Bar Mk3 knife, with serrated edge, is used by RDA personnel for self-defense and hunting.

Flamethrower
The FT-M3A1 flamethrower is scaled up for use by Recoms and Skel Suit operators.

AERIAL ASSAULT

Desperate to repel the RDA's strike on the Tree of Souls, a Na'vi warrior prepares to attack a Scorpion Gunship. The power of a Na'vi bow is so great that an arrow fired from one can even penetrate the reinforced canopy glass of an armored RDA vehicle.

RDA AND CET-OPS VEHICLES

The RDA's scaled-up territorial ambitions on Pandora require a new generation of faster and deadlier vehicles

Adapting the latest tech from a war-torn Earth to the RDA's needs in an extraterrestrial world, a new generation of land, sea, and air vehicles is deployed. These high-performance mobile machines build, patrol, and protect RDA installations across Pandora, enabling RDA expansion into new territories and additional forms of resource extraction.

Furthermore, now that the RDA has discovered *amrita*—the substance in *tulkun* brains that can halt human aging—a primary new focus is Cet-Ops (Cetacean Operations) and its aggressive, purpose-built hunting vessels, including spotter aircraft, Mako fast-attack subs, nimble Picador boats, and amphibious Crab Suit mini-subs.

AT-101 SeaWasp
This new-gen, quad-rotor aerial gunship is designed for long-range patrol and *tulkun* spotting as well as Sec-Ops escort and CAS (Close Air Support).

S-76 SeaDragon
The SeaDragon is a purpose-designed mothership for *tulkun* hunting. It deploys surface boats and hunter subs to track, harpoon, and harvest the giant beings.

SA-9 Kestrel gunship
A new-gen ducted-rotor gunship, the Kestrel is a fighting and general transport craft. Its arsenal of integrated weaponry is accompanied by two door-gun positions and a rear ramp gunner, making the craft difficult to surprise or destroy.

MISSION EQUIPMENT

As the RDA returns to Pandora, it is taking no chances against the moon's Indigenous warriors and deadly creatures. It is also throwing everything it can at the hunt for *tulkun*, although it doesn't take long for the RDA's commanding officer, Colonel Miles Quaritch, to conscript dedicated *tulkun*-hunting vessels like the S-76 SeaDragon into mission to hunt down and kill the leader of the Na'vi insurgency, Jake Sully.

Crab Suit
Operating as underwater AMPs (Amplified Mobility Platforms), Crab Suits deploy from a SeaDragon mothership to assist in the recovery of dead *tulkun* taken by the swift hunting boats and subs.

MS-3 Type 2 Mako
The Mako submersible herds *tulkun* from below. It fires harpoon torpedoes at a target animal, which inflate lift bags, forcing the *tulkun* to the water's surface for the kill.

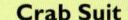

Matador
This high-speed forward command, support, and harpoon platform is quick to chase down its prey. The armory includes a depth-charge launcher, machine guns, and a harpoon launcher.

175

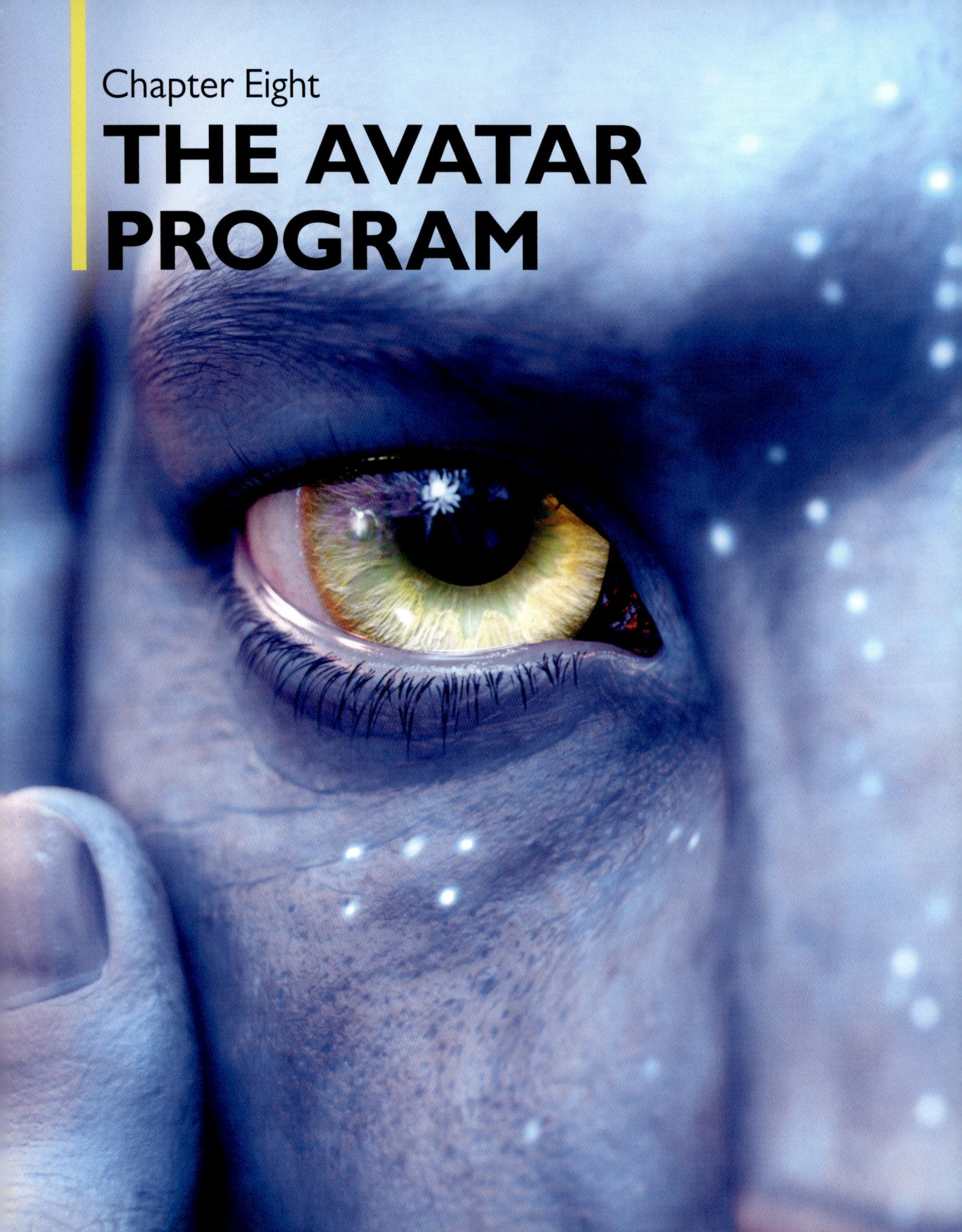

Chapter Eight
THE AVATAR PROGRAM

THE AVATAR PROGRAM

An RDA scientific breakthrough has enabled humans to thrive in Pandora's toxic atmosphere

An avatar is a biological shell—the body of a Na'vi hybridized with human DNA—that can be inhabited by a human consciousness. Avatars are invaluable on Pandora, because the Na'vi body is perfectly adapted to an environment hostile to humans. The RDA's Avatar Program was originally intended to create mineworkers who would not need to wear protective suits and could eat Pandoran foodstuffs. However, the cost of the necessary mental link system was deemed too high for the numbers of mineworkers needed.

The Avatar Program was then assigned to improve communication with the indigenous Na'vi. The program thus moved from being a poorly-defined xenobiological experiment controlled by Earth-based bureaucrats, academics, and politicians to a tightly-managed engineering project incorporating the most advanced RDA technology.

Standing tall
Program leader Dr. Grace Augustine closes the doors of the Avatar Long House where the avatars sleep. At 10 ft (3.3 m) she towers over human Sci-Ops aids.

A scientific wonder
New arrival Jake Sully discovers the work of the Avatar Program scientists. Avatars are shipped to Pandora in a nutrient-rich amnio-tank, where they grow and mature during the long journey from Earth.

GAINING A SECOND BODY

Each human volunteer is paired with their avatar—a genetically engineered human/Na'vi hybrid known as a chimera. The human controller's consciousness inhabits the avatar body via a psionic link, while their human body remains in a sleep-like state. Each individual's personality thus controls a custom-made Na'vi body. An avatar has no consciousness of its own and remains in a vegetative state when not inhabited by a human controller. A human can only inhabit an avatar with their own DNA profile, thus each avatar has a unique user.

Each cloned avatar is a genetic hybrid of a Pandoran native and a specific human, although in size and appearance the mix favors Na'vi genes. Avatars reveal their human genes by possessing five digits (as opposed to the Na'vi's four) on their hands and feet, and by the smaller size of their eyes.

Telltale eyes
Avatar bodies feature human eyebrows, a quirk of their hybrid DNA profile. This genetic giveaway is another simple way to distinguish between avatars and Na'vi.

179

SCIENCE PERSONNEL

A team of dedicated scientists works to unlock Pandora's secrets

The RDA Sci-Ops (Science Operations) division is home to the Avatar Program. In 2154, funding and staffing levels are low, as the RDA has siphoned off funds to its unobtanium mining operations. Avatar Program head Dr. Grace Augustine does all she can to keep the program running, document Pandora's flora and fauna, and maintain good relations with the Na'vi. The ongoing discourse between the Pandoran-based scientific community—who are dedicated to learning all they can about the amazing flora, fauna, and Na'vi people of the moon—and the greedy corporate interests of their RDA sponsors leads only to conflict.

Giant steps
Grace's avatar is one of the first humans to set foot on Pandora, giving her unparalleled opportunities to explore.

Dr. Grace Augustine

Grace Augustine comes to Pandora nearly three decades before conflict erupts between the Na'vi and the RDA, excited by the prospect of exploring this vibrant moon and discovering the potential benefits of its wondrous flora and fauna. She arrives as a young, respected botanist, a wunderkind in a field that has struggled to maintain viability on Earth, where the formerly great diversity of plant life has been systematically destroyed.

Grace is captivated by Pandora's fascinating ecosystem and its myriad riches. She contributes to research that results in Pandoran flora-derived cures for several common Earth viruses. She also comes to deeply appreciate the wonder and wisdom of the moon's native inhabitants, the Na'vi.

Eventually, Grace's research into Pandora's botany and the culture of the Na'vi begins to be disparaged by RDA head administrator Parker Selfridge. Fatally wounded by Colonel Quaritch after she sides with the Na'vi, Grace's avatar gives birth to a daughter named Kiri, who is later adopted by Jake and Neytiri.

Dedication personified
Grace's utter commitment to her work gives her the courage to stand up against the pressures put upon her by the RDA hierarchy.

Dr. Norm Spellman

Scientist Norm Spellman spent much of his life preparing for his journey to Pandora. An excellent student, Norm always looked to the stars as he read and re-read books written by his hero, Dr. Grace Augustine. Years of hard work bore fruit when he was accepted into the Avatar Program.

Arriving on the moon, Norm is shocked to learn of the discord between Hell's Gate's various factions. Norm works tirelessly with the Avatar team to keep his mind occupied and off of the rising tension.

Norm undergoes extreme changes during his time on Pandora, finding unexpected love and learning the true nature of the conflict between the RDA and the Na'vi. Ultimately the scientist becomes a soldier, as he assists the Omatikaya in their battle against the RDA. After the defeat of the RDA, Jake Sully makes Norm the new head of the Avatar Program, following Grace Augustine's death.

Expert guide
Norm's knowledge of Pandora is a great help to the Avatar Program Sci-Ops team when they are out in the field.

Dr. Max Patel

Grace Augustine's right hand, Dr. Max Patel is in charge of the vital Avatar Program link units and stays on Pandora after the RDA's expulsion. He prefers not to get involved in corporate conflicts or moralizing about the role of scientists on Pandora.

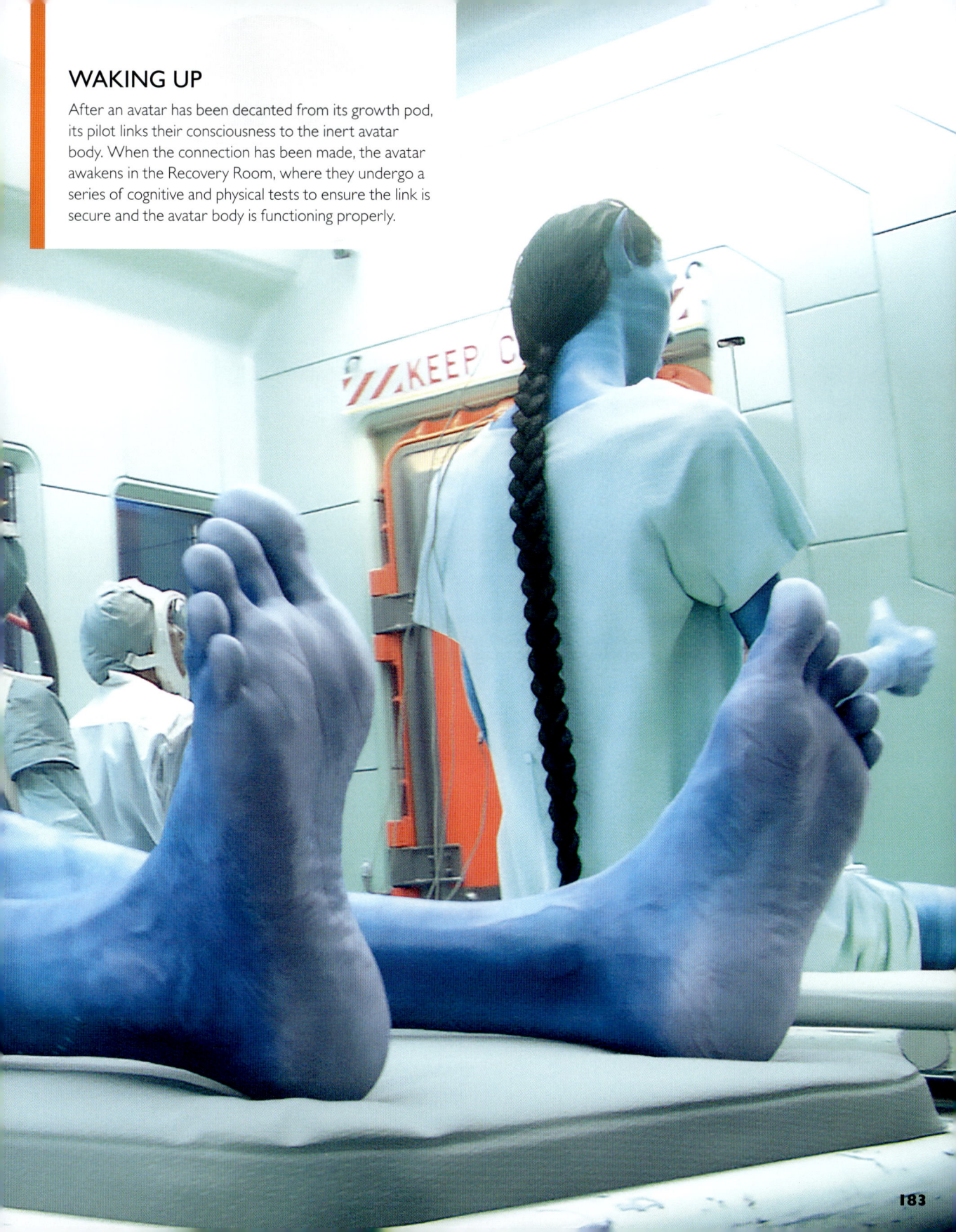

WAKING UP

After an avatar has been decanted from its growth pod, its pilot links their consciousness to the inert avatar body. When the connection has been made, the avatar awakens in the Recovery Room, where they undergo a series of cognitive and physical tests to ensure the link is secure and the avatar body is functioning properly.

SCIENCE TECHNOLOGY

High-tech equipment for all aspects of the RDA's operation: mining, security, and scientific research

By the 22nd century, human beings have learned to harness the power of superconductive materials like unobtanium and master faster-than-light space travel. They have also made technological breakthroughs that impact the personal and corporate worlds.

The RDA, the largest conglomerate business in the known universe, has spent billions of dollars creating a variety of sophisticated technological items for its military and scientific arms. Some of the RDA's most cutting-edge technology can be found on—and indeed was developed specifically for use on—Pandora. Such technology is used for mining operations, exploration, the development of the Pandoran environment, and the Avatar Program.

Heads-up displays
Trudy Chacón and members of the Avatar Program team review false color images of the Flux Vortex over the Tree of Souls.

View from inside
The RDA's HQ boasts a 3D holographic display of the landscape of Pandora, showing where key unobtanium deposits have been surveyed.

Sec-Ops & Sci-Ops equipment

Breather pack
This exo-pack is essential wear for humans in the toxic Pandoran atmosphere. Its rechargeable battery pack lasts 10 hours.

Earpiece and throat mic
For remote communication, humans and avatars wear these miniature comms to speak over long distances.

Lab workstation computer terminal
Used by Dr. Grace Augustine and the Avatar research team, these curved-screen terminals have 3D immersive displays and have workspace-sharing capabilities with the RDA datapads.

Long-range radio
When traveling across Pandora, electromagnetic Flux Vortices often interfere with radio signals. This portable, long-range radio contains tech to help resolve that issue.

Avatar Program equipment

Compass
This device is used by field operatives who are traveling light and not looking to be weighed down by heavy packs.

Binoculars
With various settings, including infrared and night vision, these binoculars enhance an avatar's already superb eyesight.

Tissue sample storage unit
Sci-Ops Avatar Program members use this unit to transport samples in the field back to Hell's Gate.

Soil sample kit
Used to collect soil samples for transport, the kit includes a root stimulus probe, a sample tool, and a PH monitor.

Aircom handset
Employed by Avatar Program field agents when deep in the rainforest, this sat-phone gives access to all signals broadcast by Hell's Gate.

HUMAN-NA'VI PROGRAMS

The return of the RDA to Pandora evolves the AVTR program amid new Na'vi resistance

After the RDA's defeat at the Battle of the Hallelujah Mountains in 2154, it takes 15 years for the organization to return to Pandora. This time a new breed of transgenic human/Na'vi hybrid warriors called Recombinants, or Recoms, has been developed. Classified as Project Phoenix, the Recom program was fully funded as part of the RDA's counteroffensive invasion force and accelerated immediately on arrival. Similar to avatar bodies, Recoms are created and grown, but, unlike avatars, they do not need a human driver to operate them from a remote location. The memories of deceased RDA Sec-Ops troopers are uploaded to the consciousness of Recombinants, so these new hybrid warriors are untethered from the need for a psionic link between human and hybrid body.

At the same time, an earlier initiative, The Ambassador Program, or TAP, which was shut down during the RDA retreat, comes back to haunt the organization when its captured Na'vi subjects emerge from cryogenic sleep. Joining the Na'vi insurgency, these disaffected young Na'vi seek to relearn their heritage, reclaim their world, and resist the human invaders.

THE AMBASSADOR PROGRAM
CONNECTING WORLDS

CULTURAL REAWAKENING

The intention of TAP, run by John Mercer, was to raise young Na'vi as humans and turn them against their own species, furthering the RDA's aims to colonize Pandora (see also pp. 86–87). With the RDA defeat in 2154, Mercer evacuated TAP and ordered the execution of the Na'vi students. However, these Na'vi were secretly put into cryogenic storage and reawakened 15 years later when the RDA returned to Pandora.

TAP poster
Propaganda is aimed at presenting TAP as beneficial to Pandora. In truth, it aimed to rob young Na'vi of their cultural ties and heritage.

Colonel Quaritch

Miles Quaritch was 51 years old when he died in the Battle of the Hallelujah Mountains on Pandora. Now his identity and memory have been uploaded into the body of a Recombinant warrior that is 9 ft 5 in (2.9 m) tall and biologically only slightly "older" than Jake Sully's avatar when he arrived on Pandora. In Quaritch, this combination of physical youth and experience of mind is highly potent and deadly. Retaining his rank of colonel, Quaritch leads a squad of 11 Recoms in a new mission: to hunt down and kill Jake Sully, the traitor to humanity and leader of the Na'vi insurgency responsible for the expulsion of the RDA from Pandora.

Back in action
In his new form as a Recom, Quaritch now feels one step closer to understanding the Na'vi.

RECOM PROGRAM

As autonomous beings, Recoms are inherently more stable and self-sustaining than avatars, representing a massive advancement in genetic engineering. Recoms have Na'vi DNA, so *Eywa* does not detect them as a threat, unlike humans and machines. This means they can walk freely through Pandora without triggering *Eywa*'s immune response (see pp. 124–25). Going undetected by *Eywa* gives Recom troops a tactical advantage in the forest: using Na'vi-like stealth, they are able to establish their own hunting ground.

Corporal Wainfleet

Originally a human AMP Suit driver and Samson gunner until his death in the Battle of the Hallelujah Mountains, Lyle Wainfleet is now reconfigured as a Recom warrior and is keen for payback on the Na'vi. Corporal Wainfleet is team leader of Colonel Quaritch's Recom unit, earning his position as a result of his diverse combat skills and bullish devotion to his fellow troopers. As an assigned Jungle Escort to the avatars in the Avatar Program, Wainfleet has had exposure to the lives of the human/Na'vi hybrids. What his former self would shrug off as "their problem" has become the intelligence and preparation he needs for life as a Recom.

Seasoned soldier
Recoms retain the tattoos they had as humans: Wainfleet has five. He is equipped with multiple firearms, as well as grenades and a machete.

187

Mansk
Like all Recom operators, Mansk fought and died in the Battle of the Hallelujah Mountains before being resurrected.

RECOM EQUIPMENT

The hardware necessary for subduing the Pandoran rainforest and its inhabitants

The Recoms' mission is facilitated by a range of tools, weapons, firearms, and artillery that aids their survival in the often-hostile Pandoran environment. These operators are equipped to achieve their mission by any means necessary and to ensure the RDA's advancement and its military goal: to retake Pandora in order to provide a new home for humanity. The RDA believes that every living being on Pandora wants to repulse it, and the Recoms must be aware of that fact every second of every day.

Field gear

Team badge
The motto, "We will tread on you," promotes the "unstoppable force" of the Recom front line.

Hydration pack
This field canteen contains anticontaminant filters to supply safe, drinkable water.

Breather
The AAS-R02 atmos adaptation system provides carbon dioxide to Recom personnel inside human-air facilities.

Throat comms
This comms belt and mic is equipped with "push to talk" and atmos capable speakers.

Weapons

Recom weapons are versions of the artillery units used by the human Skel Suit platform, modified and adjusted for the Recom physiology.

Z-33R pistol
Scaled to Recom size (R), this standard-issue pistol fires up to 40 rounds a minute.

Frag grenades
Fragmentation grenades disperse high-velocity shards upon detonation.

Assault rounds
0226-LSAR (Linkable Skel Assault Round) ammunition fragments upon impact, causing maximum devastation.

Recom combat/utility knife
The sawteeth, or serrations, on the back of this knife (also shown in sheath) can be used to cut Pandoran rainforest branches or weaken them for easier breaking.

RECOM M69-AR
The M69-AR is chambered in .50 caliber BAT (Battalion, Anti-Tank) to pack a much larger punch than smaller, human-scaled weapons.

Recom Hydra machine gun
The Recom variant of the earlier, mounted .50 caliber Hydra machine gun is held like a standard firearm.

Walker
Recom operator Walker dies for a second time during her second tour of Pandora.

Chapter Nine

NEW CHALLENGES

BRIDGEHEAD: A NEW COMMUNITY

Pandora's first human settlement promises a new chapter for the people of a ravaged Earth

Bridgehead is now transformed from a dirt-laden construction site into a system of paved roads and fortified edifices. Its factories, refineries, fusion powerplant, and cooling towers define the skyline, with dry docks and shipyards where massive vessels for the industrial-scale harvesting of *tulkun amrita* are constructed.

Bridgehead's thousands of workers and residents live in dormitary housing that sprawls around central, semi-mercantile pedestrian zones. The RDA's plan is to shape a functioning city center for Bridgehead, complete with appealing suburban houses, community centers, indoor and outdoor sports facilities, and retail zones, which will offer humanity back on ravaged Earth the promise of a new life in Pandora. At the same time, the Na'vi continue to wear down the RDA by attacking RDA maglev trains, mining operations, and pipelines around Bridgehead.

Industrial workhorse
An RDA construction blimp hovers over Bridgehead. These low-speed, heavy-lift platforms are used for such tasks as transportation and aerial pesticide spraying.

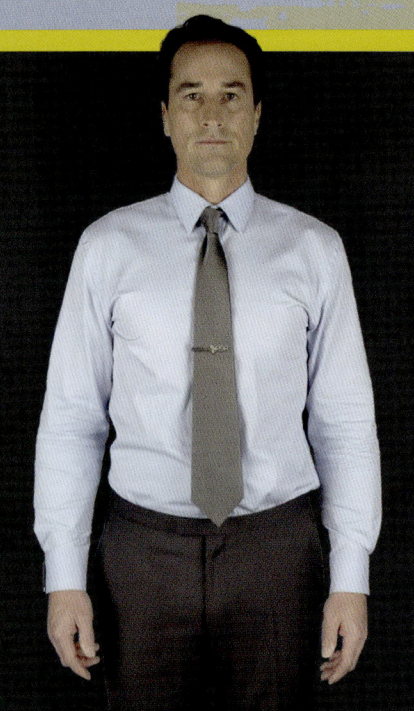

New manager
Parker Selfridge's replacement as the RDA's head administrator on Pandora, Charlies Stringer oversees the management of Bridgehead operations. Over years, he has gained the trust of the RDA leadership, always prioritizing their needs and achieving the results they demand without question. That is what he does best: upholding power structures.

Office worker
Stringer prefers to stay within walking distance of his office at the Ops Center in Bridgehead and away from the dangers of Pandora.

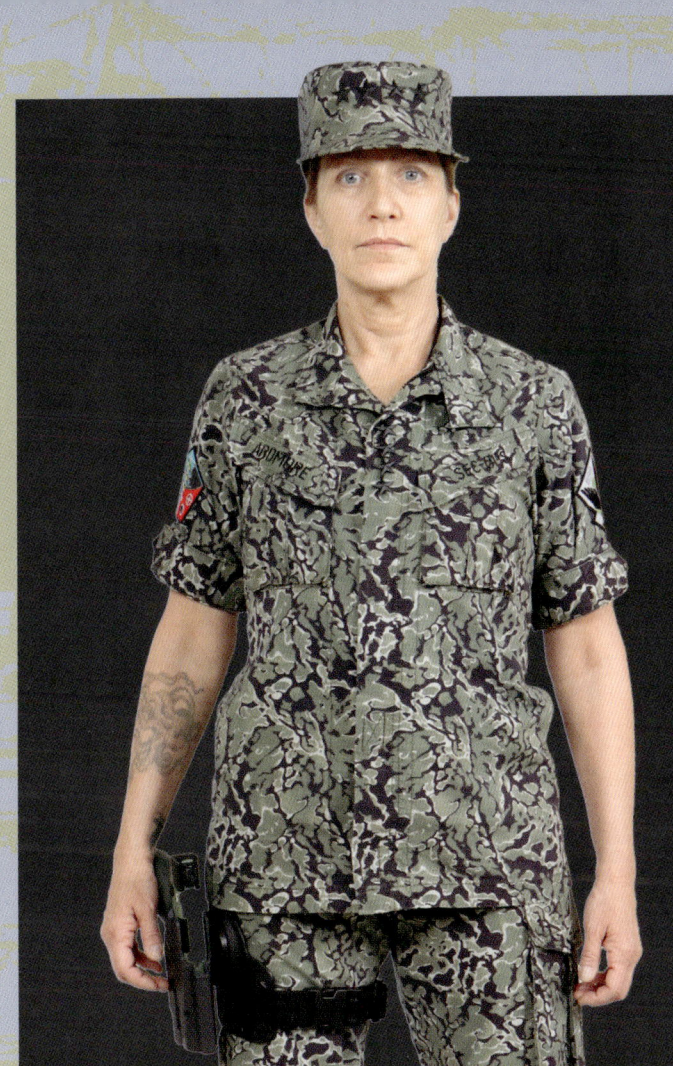

Military mind

General Ardmore has been effective in getting Bridgehead up and running, earning the respect of the RDA leadership and its shareholders. She is more determined than ever to capture Jake Sully, but is not convinced when Colonel Quaritch enlists the help of the Ash People to track him down. She continues to believe Pandora can be taken by sheer military force and has no plan for combating the moon's immune response—triggered when the RDA began building Bridgehead.

Frustrated tactician
Ardmore believes that her strategies succeed and that she always comes out on top.

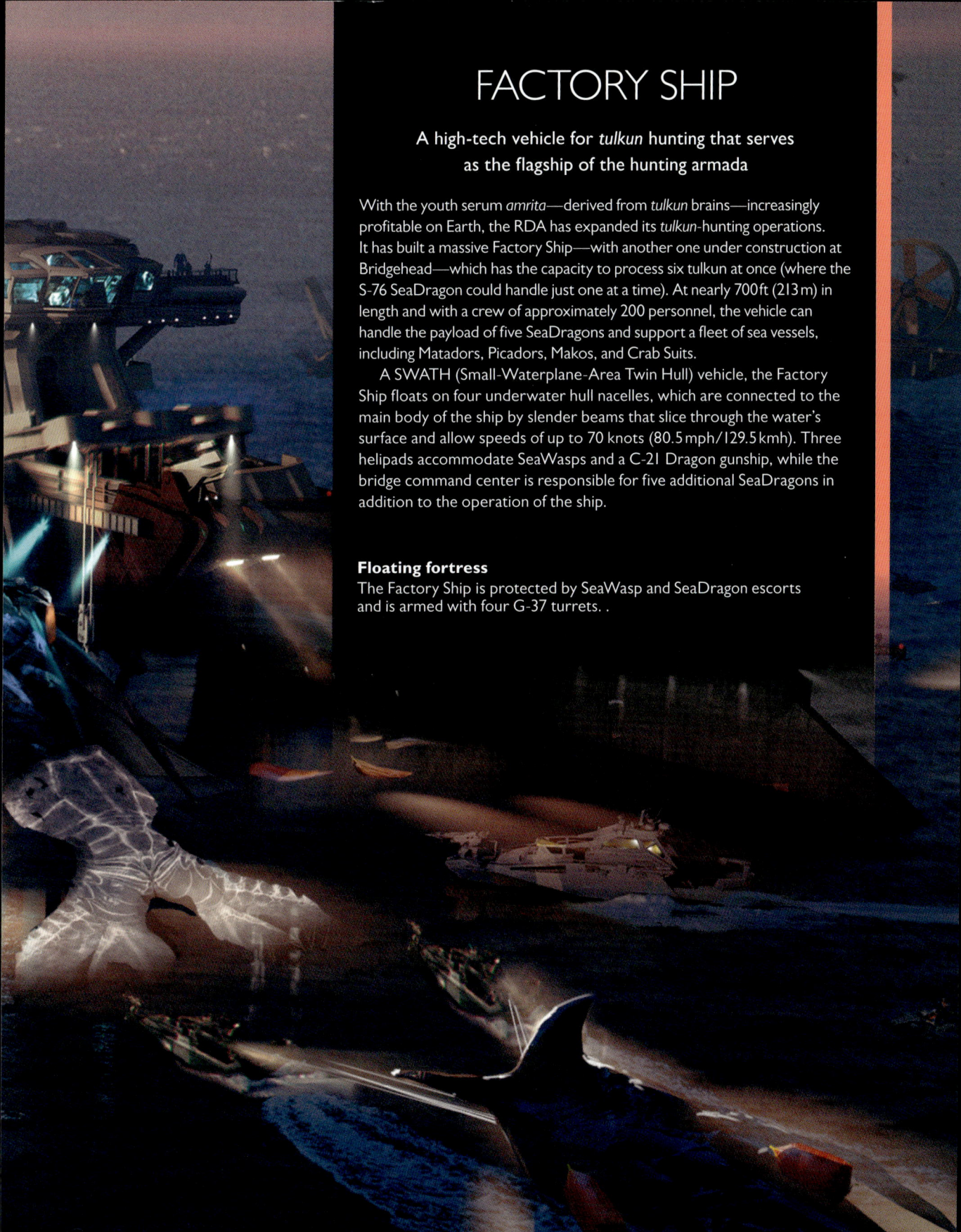

FACTORY SHIP

A high-tech vehicle for *tulkun* hunting that serves as the flagship of the hunting armada

With the youth serum *amrita*—derived from *tulkun* brains—increasingly profitable on Earth, the RDA has expanded its *tulkun*-hunting operations. It has built a massive Factory Ship—with another one under construction at Bridgehead—which has the capacity to process six tulkun at once (where the S-76 SeaDragon could handle just one at a time). At nearly 700ft (213m) in length and with a crew of approximately 200 personnel, the vehicle can handle the payload of five SeaDragons and support a fleet of sea vessels, including Matadors, Picadors, Makos, and Crab Suits.

A SWATH (Small-Waterplane-Area Twin Hull) vehicle, the Factory Ship floats on four underwater hull nacelles, which are connected to the main body of the ship by slender beams that slice through the water's surface and allow speeds of up to 70 knots (80.5mph/129.5kmh). Three helipads accommodate SeaWasps and a C-21 Dragon gunship, while the bridge command center is responsible for five additional SeaDragons in addition to the operation of the ship.

Floating fortress
The Factory Ship is protected by SeaWasp and SeaDragon escorts and is armed with four G-37 turrets. .

A BATTLE FOR SURVIVAL

The fate of Pandora itself is at stake as tensions flare in a battle for survival between cultures

With the strengthening of the human foothold on Pandora and the growing threat to ancestral lands caused by the spread of development, the Na'vi prepare for the inevitable escalation of war. They have many questions to answer. Should they arm themselves with human weapons or hold fast to "The Na'vi Way"? Can the clans unite into a force capable of driving out the RDA? Will relentless guerilla action wear down the corporation until it loses the economic ability to press for colonization? Overall, the Na'vi remain hopeful that one day Pandora will return to its peaceful way of life.

Hope on the wing
Just as Pandora's environments, from its swamplands (shown here) to its rainforests, continually rejuvenate themselves, the Na'vi will never cease defending their beautiful home world.

Strength in unity
In the spirit of Jake Sully's belief that "Family is our fortress," the Na'vi clans are increasingly seeking to unite in resisistance to the might of the RDA.

INDEX

A

akula **65**, 81
Akwey 117
Alira 115
Alpha Centauri Expeditions (ACE) 87, 163
AMP (Amplified Mobility Platform) Suit 142, 143, 155, 160, **162-165**, 166, 169, 175, 187
amrita 13, 70, 157, 174, 192, 195
anemonoid **28**, 60-61
Angat 120
Anufi 118
Anurai clan 42, 47, **116**
Ao'Nung 106, 107
arachnoid 42, **44**, 83
Aranahe clan 22, 23, 59, **119**
Ardmore, Francis **157**, 192
Asahe 119
atokirina 125, 126, 129
atoll **20-21**, 104, 106, 121
Augustine, Dr. Grace 26, 35, 85, 87, 91, 94, 95, 101, 154, 178, 180-181, 185
austrapede 44
Avatar Program 145, 155, **178-179**, 180-183, 184-187
  RDA avatars 75, 182-183
  Recoms 121, 154-155, 157, 186-189
Awa'atlu 108

B

banshee of paradise 29
banshee's tail 31
beetlehorn ursabrute 47
binary sunshine 28
bladeheads 22
"Blue Flute Clan" 91
blood urchin 31
Bridgehead 140, **148-149** 150-151, 192-193, 195
buoyfish 64

C

canalyd 28
cannonball tree 27
cat ear 28
celia fruit tree 26
Chacón, Trudy **155**, 184
chalice plant 28
chameleon crawler 46
chandelier fish 65
cillaphant 29
cloaked panther 46
cloud spitter 30

Clouded Forest 22, 23, 30, 31, 46, 58, 118
Cove of the Ancestors **14**, 83, 135
crested porcubear **42**
cuirass crab **44**, 116
cuirass mud crab **44**

D

daisy anemone 68
dakteron 28
dinicthoid 60, 61
direhorse 19, **40-41**, 53, 75, 91, 117, 118
dragon mushroom 31
Dream Hunt 44, 78, 79, 83

E

Eastern Sea 108, 114, 121
echo stalker 23, 46
Entu 86, **93**, 119
episoth tree 26
Etuwa 119
eyethorn 31
Eytukan 78, 92, 93, 94
Eywa 13, 20, 50, 75, 76, 78, 82-83, 87, 92, 95, 106, 112, 113, 114, 116, 119, 124-125, 126, 128-129, 130, 132, 135, 187

F

fan lizard 28, **44**
fantail coral 69
feather blade 30
feathertail fish 63
First Songs 76, 86
flaska reclinata 29
flat skate fish 63
flux pinning 14
Flux Vortex 14, 184
fountain tree 27

G

giant ilu 65
gill mantle 62
glider fin 63
goblin thistle 29
great austrapede 45
great leonopteryx (*toruk*) **50-51**, 56, 57, 75, 86, 93, 115
Grinder, the 160
grub plant 28

H

Hallelujah Mountains 14, **16-17**, 52, 53, 93, 94, 95, 100, 101, 121, 140, 155, 156, 166, 186, 187, 188
hammerbrow fish **63**
hammerhead titanothere 19, 23, **38-39**, 44, 155
Harding, Angela **156**
Havang 120
Hawnutu'un 121
helicoradian 19, **28**
helidais mushroom 31
Hell's Gate 19, 94, 140, 142, **144-145**, 147, 148, 154, 155, 160, 168, 169, 181, 185
hellfire wasp 56, **57**
hellhound 171
hexbot 148, 150, 151, 152-153
hexapede 23, **42**, 57, 103
High Camp 95, **100-101**
Highlands 120, 135
Hometree 18, 50, 52, 78, 79, 82, 83, 86, 91, 92, 94, **96-99**, 112, 113, 119, 120, 154, 159
Hulanta clan **120**, 135
hydrogen sulfide 13, 29

I

Ikeyni 114
Iknimaya 17, 52, 54
ilu 4, **63**, 65, 104, 108
ISV *Venture Star* **138-139**
ISV *Manifest Destiny* 140

K

Kame'tire clan 22, **118**
Kanat 119
Kekunan clan 115
Kinglor Forest 22, **23**, 59, 119
kinglor 23, **59**, 119
Kiri 94, **95**, 180
kite manta 59
kuru 41, 42, 53, 62, 63, 70, 75, 129, 130, 135

L

leaf pitcher 28
lift vine 30
Liquid Environment Transport 161
lizard tree 27
Lo'ak 94, **95**

M

malmok (Rings of Stone) 15
Mansk 188
marui 100, 108, 109
Mangkwan clan 58, **112-113**
medusoid **59**, 110-111, 112
Mercer, John 119, 156, 164, 165, 186
mermaid tail 30
Metkayina clan 14, 20, 21, 22, 67, 70, 80, 81, 82, 83, 84, 95, **104-109**, 121, 135
Minang 118
mist bloom 30
Mo'at **92**, 93, 95, 125
Mokasa 118
Mons Veritatis 52, 100

moonroll 64
mountain banshee (*ikran*) 16, 17, 21, 31, 37, 50, **52-53**, 54, 55, 56, 57, 58, 75, 78, 79, 82, 86, 91, 97, 100, 104, 110-111, 114, 115, 117, 160
mudcrawler 65

N

nalutsa 60
Na'ring 19
Na'vi 12, 13, 16, 17, 23, 26-28, 30, 31, 48, **74-87**, 96, 97, 100, 114-121, 154, 155
  history 84-85, **86-87**
  language 50, 78, **84-85**
  physiology 45, 63, **74-75**, 106, 178-179
  religion **124-125**
  rites 17, 50, 51, 52, 54, **82-83**, 128-129
  society 20, 40, 41, 42, 60, 70-71, **76-77**, 80-81, **90-121**, 180-181, 186-187
  weapons 60, **78-79**, 113, 118, 173
Nesim 118
Neteyam 94-95, 107
Neytiri 51, 53, 92, 75, 78, 85, **92-93**, 94-95, 106, 124, 125, 131, 154, 180
nightwraiths 58-59
Nom's delight coral 69

O

oceans 68, 69, 70, 71, **80-81**
octofin fish 65
Olangi clan 117
olo'eyktan (also *olo'eykte*) 83, 92, 93, 94, 106, 111, 114, 117, 118, 119, 120, 121
Omatikaya clan 18, 19, 20, 21, 22, 35, 50, 52, 53, 54, 57, 67, 82, 85, 86, 87, **90-93**, 94, 95, 96, 97, 100, 101, **102-103**, 114, 117, 119, 121, 125, 130, 135, 156, 169, 181

P

Pandora **12-13**, 14, 15, 16, 17, 18, 19, 20, 21, 26, 28, 29, 38, 42, 44, 45, 47, 50, 53, 56, 57, 59, 60, 61, 63, 67, 68, 71, 74, 75, 76, 78, 84, 85, 86, 87, 91, 92, 93, 94, 95, 96, 103, 108, 114, 116, 120, 124, 126, 129, 138, 139, 140, 145, 148, 154, 155, 156, 160, 161, 163, 178, 179, 180, 181, 184, 186, 187, 188, 189, 192, 193, 196, 197
panopyra 19, **26**
Patel, Dr. Max 100, 181
Peylak 111
phalanxia 31
pincer fish 63
plants 18-19, **28-29**, 30-31
Polyphemus 12, 14, 16
prolemuris 42, **45**

Q

Quaritch, Colonel Miles 121, **154**, 155, 157, 160, 169, 170, 175, 180, 187, 192

R

radar mushroom 31
rain thistle 31
Ralu 86, **93**

razor palm 27
RDA 14, 20, 22, 51, 52, 56, 67, 71, 85, 87, 92, 93, 94, 95, 96, 97, 100, 101, 106, 117, 118, 119, 120, 121, 129, 131, **136-175**, 178, 184-185
  Cet-Ops 174-175
  CON-DEV 141, 148, 150
  equipment 138, 141, 143, 144-145, 148, 150-151, 155, 170, 185, 188
  military vehicles 138, 140, 142-143, 155, 157, **160-161**, 174-175, 195
  Sci-Ops 149, 155, 178, 180-181, 185
  Sec-Ops 119, 141, 145, 148, 149, 154, 155, 157, 160, 169, 170, 174, 186
  spacecraft 138, 140, 142-143
  weapons 167, **168-171**, 189
reef tick 61
Rey'tanu clan **120**, 135
rockbeak fish 64
Ronal 106, 107
Rotxo 107

S

sagittaria **60**, 61
sailfin goliath 23, 46
Saotun 120
Sarentu clan 22, **119**, 125, 156
Scoresby, Mick 157
Scorpion Gunship 155, **160**, 172-173
scorpion thistle 29
Selfridge, Parker **154**, 155, 180
Shaman of Songs 87, **93**
shimmyfly 56, **57**
shroud 58
Skel Suit **166-167**, 170, 171, 189
skimwing **62**, 66-67, 81, 106
"Sky People" 19, 20, 76, 87, 92, 100, 118
slinger 42
slinth 43
So'lek 121
songcords **77**, 80
soundblast colossus 47
spade wing 64
Spellman, Dr. Norm 100, 155, **181**
Spider 94, **95**
Spirit Tree 83, 120, **134-135**
squid fruit tree 27, 102
squid lantern 64
starbeak 64
starry doughnut coral 69
stingbat 56, **57**, 169
stormglider 59
Stringer, Charles 193
sturmbeest 42, **43**, 44, 48-49, 54, 61, 101, 102
Sully, Jake 16, 35, 38, 51, 53, 67, 87, 91, 92, 93, **94**, 95, 100, 101, 105-109, 121, 157, 175, 179, 180, 181, 187, 192, 197
sunflower gigantus 30
Sylwanin 92, **93**, 131
Syringil 64

T

Ta'unui clan **121**
tapirus 42, **45**
Tarsem 93
tarsyu 125
Tawkami clan 86, **115**
Tayrangi clan 82, **114**, 115
tetrapteron 19, **56**, 57

thanator **34-35**, 37, 42, 75
thistle bud 28
Tiaru 120
Time of First Songs 76
Tipani clan 116
Tlalim clan 59, **110-111**
Tonowari 106, 107
Toruk Makto 51, 86, 87, 93, 114, 115, 119, 121
Tree of Souls 51, 82, 117, 124, 125, 126, **128-129**, 135, 155, 173, 184
Tree of Voices 93, **130-133**, 135
Trr'ong clan 121
tsaheylu 40, 53, 75
tsahik 83, 85, 92, 93, 95, 106, 107, 113, 116, 118, 119, 120, 121, 125, 129
tsakarem 94
Tsireya 106, **107**
Tsu'tey 87, 92, 93, 94, 131
Tsyal 86, 115
Tuktirey 94-95
tulkun **70-71**, 82, 83, 84, 104, 107, 157, 166, 174, 175, 192, 195
turtapede 60, **61**
twisted lily 28

U

unidelta tree 26
unobtanium 13, 14, **15**, 16, 17, 28, 87, 96, 129, 135, 138, 143, 144, 145, 154, 155, 184
Upper Plains **22**, 23, 30, 31, 46, 47, 118
Utility Suit ("Ute suit") 163

V

Valke 115
Valkyrie Shuttle **142-143**, 146-147
Valley of Mo'ara 87
Varang 113
vein pod 29
viperwolf 19, **36-37**, 42, 154

W

Wainfleet, Corporal Lyle **155**, 187
Walker 189
warbonnet fern 19, **28**
Western Frontier **22**, 23, 30, 31, 46, 47, 59, 65, 81, 118, 121, 125, 156, 164
Wetlands 120, 135
windrays 59, 110-111
wolf tick 44

Z

zakru **47**, 118
Zeswa clan 22, 118

Senior Editor Craig Jelley
Senior Designer Jon Hall
Cover Design LLÖ
Production Editor Siu Yin Chan
Senior Production Controller Mary Slater
Managing Editor Emma Grange
Managing Art Editor Vicky Short
Art Director Charlotte Coulais
Managing Director Mark Searle

Written for DK by Joshua Izzo, Reymundo Perez and Simon Beecroft
Designed for DK by LLÖ

DK would like to thank: James Cameron, Jon Landau, Joshua Izzo, Reymundo Perez, Ben Procter, Dylan Cole, Deborah L. Scott, Joseph C. Pepe, Zachary Berger, Hana Scott-Suhrstedt, Shealyn Biron, Fausto De Martini, Jonathan Berube, Aashrita Kamath, Sasha De Mello, Alex Wolff, Jeff Reeves, Lisa Fitzpatrick, Danny Shelby, Kathy Franklin, LeAnne Arnold, Anneke Suyderhoud, and Zachary Kennedy at Lightstorm; Carol Roeder and Nicole Spiegel at 20th Century Studios, and Julia March for proofreading. For their work on the previous edition: Alastair Dougall, Nathan Martin, Beth Davies, Jenny Edwards, Toby Truphet, Sarah Harland, Jo Connor, Julie Ferris, and Thomas Hoeler.

This edition published in 2025
First published in Great Britain in 2022 by
Dorling Kindersley Limited
20 Vauxhall Bridge Road,
London SW1V 2SA

The authorised representative in the EEA is
Dorling Kindersley Verlag GmbH. Arnulfstr. 124,
80636 Munich, Germany

Copyright © Dorling Kindersley Limited.
A Penguin Random House Company
10 9 8 7 6 5 4 3 2 1
001–354800–Nov/2025

© 2025 20th Century Studios.

All rights reserved.
No part of this publication may be reproduced, stored in or introduced into a retrieval system, or transmitted, in any form, or by any means (electronic, mechanical, photocopying, recording, or otherwise), without the prior written permission of the copyright owner. DK values and supports copyright. Thank you for respecting intellectual property laws by not reproducing, scanning or distributing any part of this publication by any means without permission. By purchasing an authorised edition, you are supporting writers and artists and enabling DK to continue to publish books that inform and inspire readers.
No part of this publication may be used or reproduced in any manner for the purpose of training artificial intelligence technologies or systems. In accordance with Article 4(3) of the DSM Directive 2019/790, DK expressly reserves this work from the text and data mining exception.

A CIP catalogue record for this book
is available from the British Library.
ISBN 978-0-2417-7718-3

Printed and bound in China

www.dk.com
www.avatar.com

This book was made with Forest Stewardship Council™ certified paper – one small step in DK's commitment to a sustainable future. Learn more at www.dk.com/uk/information/sustainability